Habakkuk

A Prophecy For Our Time

Edition 01-Revision 10

Bible Book 35 of 66

Victor Robert Farrell

Habakkuk

A Prophecy For Our Time

Bible Book 35 of 66

All current

Contact & Sales Information

Can be found at

www.TheologyShop.com

Habakkuk

A Prophecy For Our Time

Bible Book 35 of 66

Copyright © Rev. Victor Robert Farrell

ISBN Number 978-0-9538864-3-2

First published

February 2014 by Whispering Word

All current contact and sales information can be found at

www.TheologyShop.com

Printed in The United Kingdom

for

WhisperingWord

Habakkuk

A Prophecy For Our Time

Bible Book 35 of 66

Dedication

This book is dedicated, very simply,

To the now four most important people

In the whole wide world to me.

My daughter Gemma,

My son Jonathan,

My grandaughter Ellie May,

And of course,

My wife

Bridget.

Grammar, Bible Versions & WARNINGS!

To be British, is to be somewhat like 'the last of the Mohicans.' The Britain, that is, the United Kingdom I grew up in is breaking apart. No, sadly, it is broken and never to be repaired. Even so, I am of Irish & Scottish great-grandparents, grandparents and parents, and I was also born in England. Therefore, I am British and a Celt at that. In addition to this, I love North America and the South in particular, so much so, that I feel like a British Red-Neck. Does this make me a Yankophile, or loving the South in particular (and its battle flag) does it make me more especially a Dixiophile? Alternatively, maybe I could be an Americophile or a Canameriphile? Who knows? Suffice to say, that as our nations were once only divided by a common 'English' language, (America still being the residence of the majority of our English readers,) I have tried to adopt the spelling and grammar of the Americas. In this, I have no doubt failed, and in the so doing, both mixed and matched the UK and US spelling and English grammatical styles. In doing this, I confess that I am a double-minded man, and unstable in all my editorial ways. The purists, either side of the pond, I am sure will never forgive me. The rest do not care. Either way, I need your help. So, if you spot any 'howlers,' do let me know. Email me your corrections on,

getyouracttogetherman@whisperingword.com

BIBLE VERSIONS

Ah, the Bible. The true meta-narrative of the real world and therefore all things meta-physical. Well, preferring the 'Textus Receptus' or the 'Majority Text,' I have tried to use the New Separatist Bible (NSB), which is a confluence Bible based on the 1560 Geneva Bible and the 1611 Authorized version, (Pure Cambridge Edition) when I have referenced the Bible, though where necessary, for mere contemporary clarity of course, when I have I have deviated from this norm, at that time I have clearly indicated which other Bible Version has been referenced.

JUST A HUCKSTER

Some young preacher will study until he has to get thick glasses to take care of his failing eyesight because he has an idea he wants to become a famous preacher. HE'S JUST A HUCKSTER buying selling and getting gain. They will ordain him and he will be known as Reverend and if he writes a book, they will make him a doctor. And he will be known as Doctor; but he's still a huckster buying and selling and getting gain.

**And when the Lord comes back,
HE will drive him out of the temple
along with the other cattle.**

A.W. Tozer

(from 'Tozer on Christian Leadership,' compiled by Ron Eggert)

John 3:30 *He must increase
but I must decrease.*

STILL LOOKING

Wise men speak of trees
From the Cedar to the Hyssop
Springing from the wall
From the Aspen to the Alder
Beside the water fall

Wise men speak of animals of creeping things and fish
Of birds and bees and smooth black cats
That lap the dainty dish

Wise men sing of love and capture moments in a jar
Wise men suck the juice of days
Wise men shop at Spar

Wise men count the fallen ticks
Of old clocks running down
Wise men number muscles
That help create the frown

Wise men follow after
Wise men follow far
Wise men seek the Savior still
Beneath the wandering star

1 Kings 4:33 Also he spoke of trees, from the cedar tree of Lebanon even to the hyssop that springs out of the wall; he spoke also of animals, of birds, of creeping things, and of fish. (NKJV)

THE OLD 100TH!

All people that on earth do dwell,
Sing to the Lord with cheerful voice.
Him serve with fear, His praise forth tell;
Come ye before Him and rejoice.

The Lord, ye know, is God indeed;
Without our aid He did us make;
We are His folk, He doth us feed,
And for His sheep He doth us take.

O enter then His gates with praise;
Approach with joy His courts unto;
Praise, laud, and bless His name always,
For it is seemly so to do.

For why? the Lord our God is good;
His mercy is for ever sure;
His truth at all times firmly stood,
And shall from age to age endure.

To Father, Son and Holy Ghost,
The God whom Heaven and earth adore,
From men and from the angel host
Be praise and glory evermore.

From 'Fourscore and Seven Psalms of David'
(Geneva, Switzerland: 1561); attributed to William Kethe

PREFACE

Written by Pastor, Rev. Victor Robert Farrell, the Everyday Bible Insights called 'Night Whispers' have long since been a global endeavor in communicating the God of the whole Bible in raw terms to real people. This is the passion of V.R. and the reason why he remains CEO of The 66 Books Ministry, who, through their 66 Cities project, over the course of 25 years, by the grace of God and according to His will and favor, shall be preaching consecutively from each of the 66 Books of the Holy Bible, the Gospel of the Lord Jesus Christ in 16,500 of the most influential cities of the world on an ongoing and annual basis!

Drawn from the 'Night Whispers' compilations, 'Habakkuk - A Prophecy For Our Time' is a collection of Everyday Bible Insights focusing solely on the 35th book of the Holy Bible and the 8th book of the Minor prophets, the prophecy of Habakkuk.

The Bible Insights contained in this collection are not 'day specific' and so can be read whenever you please, whether consecutively or just dipped into.

V.R., along with the team at The 66 Books Ministry and Whispering Word hope and pray that these particular Everyday Bible Insights will be an enormous blessing to you in revealing just a little more, the God of the whole Bible.

Rev. Victor Robert Farrell, June 2019 Scotland

PROLOGUE

As the idolatrous nation of Judah now lived well across the covenant breaking demarcation line, the judgment of God was already swiftly on the wing and making its way toward them. Soon and very soon, Nebuchadnezzar, chief bad guy of the Babylon Empire, would destroy them and scour the land of their filth, force marching the remnant and what was left of the useful, the great and the good back to Babylon for a 70 year prison sentence.

Make no mistake about it, this judgment was 'beyond brutal' and God chose a Levitical singer, a musical composer, a passionate and dramatic Hebrew 'Celt' called Habakkuk to give his remnant a cuddle! Now, I am not talking about a 'There, there, there, poor sweet baby, let me put a plaster on your poor little scuffed knee' kind of an embrace, but rather, the kind of fearful grip that a father would use to envelope to his heart and to his protective chest his beloved children, as the bombs fell around them and hot shrapnel cut through the air.

In this year of our Lord, 2014, as the church in the West is found to be mostly dead and covered with Laodicean lukewarm vomit, as The Lord, slips the dead thing silently over the side of the storm tossed ship into the dark oblivion of the waves of secular humanism and rising Islam, what remains will need to be fortified with steel to live in a quickly changing anti-Christian world of persecution.

There is no better prophecy more equipped to speak to such a remnant who shall be so very besieged.

Welcome to Habakkuk, 35 of 66, a prophecy for our time

Bible Insight 01

When a man's madness was turned to music

Habakkuk is no insightful 'deducer' of present circumstance, he is no futurist 'perceiver' of coming possibility; he is a 'seer;' a man of God granted painful future sight. Yes, either in dream or in vision, Habakkuk is shown a coming horror movie, a film so vicious, so fearful, that it keeps him awake at night and through his long and burdensome days, bends his knees in complaining prayer, the volume of which seemed to increase in logarithmic decibels, all directly related to God's seeming lack of response.

Habakkuk 1:1

The burden which the prophet Habakkuk saw;
NKJV

In other words, the more God seemingly declined an answer to Habakkuk's prayer, the more the volume of the prophet's pleadings increased, and to such a volume, that the sound barrier of the spiritual environmental noise levels were left smashed in pieces on heaven's front porch. This pleading appeared to force God to finally come to His door, only to then dump six more carrier bags full of cinemascope full color Chaldean violent 'slasher' movie, into the shocked and open hands of the much troubled seer, with a now further command to: 'watch closely now, and write an honest and no holds barred movie review' concerning that which God was about to release.

Now then, how is your prayer life? Now then, my friend, and to you who still keep asking for this particular gift, do you still want to be a prophet? No. I didn't think so.

As requested by God, in response to these malevolent movies from the Most High, Habakkuk's cacophonic and conclusive written review contained such powerful, such awful, such majestic and moving, fabulous and fantastic observations on God, his nation, and his own calling as a prophet and a man of faith, that in the end, the prophecy could only be rightly expressed and communicated as a stunning symphony, which was accompanied by a fully tuned up professional orchestra, all attacking their instruments in full and vigorous volume, and in the so doing, Habakkuk delivered a film score which would make even Scorcese weep. (see Habbakuk 1:3)

> *Why do You show me iniquity,*
> *And cause* **me** *to see trouble?*
> *For plundering and violence* **are** *before me;*
> *There is strife, and contention arises.*

Little is heard in the Scriptures of the 'seers sheer delight in delivering a tasty little talk on God,' however, much do the Scriptures speak about the prophetic burden, you know, that weight, that knee squatting exertion of iron, all pumped heavenward; and of the pregnant pain of pictures convulsed, that will only disappear in the delivery of the same. Note then, that the prophets of God are the pumping poets of the Most High, they are the poorly paid members of heaven's Public Broadcasting Service, painting pictures with words, whilst frothing at the mouth in unkempt discomfort, wet with sweat, wrestling with God; walking with a hammer in one hand, and a chisel in the other, winding their way through the earth, drunk with pain and carrying a paint brush and a pallet knife in their back pocket, whilst all the while swaying over the face of their blotted journal which has been pierced with broken nibs that indented hard words on sermon notes now bathed in hot salt tears.

TALKS! "Come and hear our talk!" "There will be a brief talk on the Bible!" Man – for I refuse to call you a 'man of God' – Man! If all you can do on a Sunday is deliver a tame and timid talk, then you may as well go buy yourself a feather duster, a furry top hat, a pair of buck teeth and coat made of budgie feathers! For all you are, is a comedian; a joke, an amateur of letters and feathers.

So, tell me Pastor, yes, speak to me preacher, what is the atmosphere of your study? What is the aroma of your place of work? How replete with blood-bought Holy Spirit, caught and prayed over arrows, is your quivering Lord's Day message? No. I didn't think so.

TALKS! "Come and hear our talk!" "There will be a brief talk on the Bible!" Man – for I refuse to call you a 'man of God' – Man! If all you can do on a Sunday is deliver a tame and timid talk, then you may as well go buy yourself a feather duster, a furry top hat, a pair of buck teeth and coat made of budgie feathers! For all you are, is a comedian; a joke, an amateur of letters and feathers.

Church! My dear hungry friends, we need to pray that God would make our preachers men with a burden! Even men with a message from the Most High God, and I tell you this for nothing Christian: If all you are getting on a Sunday is a piece of dry bread on your dry hungry table, then I counsel you to stay in bed, for the comedy is always better when it's delivered via cable.

Listen: *The burden against the Valley of Vision. What ails you now, that you have all gone up to the housetops, You who are full of noise, A tumultuous city, a joyous city? Your slain men are not slain with the sword, Nor dead in battle. All your rulers have fled together; They are captured by the archers. All who are found in you are bound together; They have fled from afar. Therefore I said, "Look away from me, I will weep bitterly; Do not labor to comfort me Because of the plundering of the daughter of my people." Isaiah 22:1-4 NKJV*

Pray: Lord, send your men to the coal face of the study, to the hot stoves of heaven's kitchen, that they might bring us back some coal for our cold hearts and some hot food for our cold and empty souls. Lord Your church is hungry! Send us some battle chefs into the field to feed Your sheep once more. Amen and let it be so.

Bible Insight 02

How to get God's ears to wiggle once more

So, Habakkuk is I think now very tired of his desperate and repetitious double barreled prayer for mercy and deliverance. However, there are two further parts to his three sectioned open question to God, the second part being: "O Lord, how long shall I cry, And You will not hear."

Habakkuk 1:2

O Lord, how long shall I cry, And You will not hear? Even cry out to You "Violence!" And You will not save. NKJV

Now, we know that God knows and hears all things, but this 'not hearing' which Habakkuk refers to here is in fact a 'not responding to calls for mercy.' Yes, it is not only a recognition of the un-cupped nature of God's right hand from His once 'leaning over to listen' head, but a testimony of the erecting of the high gates of indignation around the once warm entrance to the ever loving wiggling of the rabbit ears of God. Interestingly, these high barred gates of indignation now set up around the ears of God, have been cast in the forges of Judah's own rebellion and 'FEDEXED' to heaven on the back of a 'poo-brown' truck called 'arrogance.' God was not listening and their pride was the problem.

The new covenant good news is this: that 'Repentance', that armored car of God's grace in Christ Jesus, can bust open those gates of God's indignation against our sin and our own pride, forever!

So, if you are groping in a noon day discomfort of a seemingly disinterested and unheeding God: then maybe you should repent of your sin? Yes, if you find yourself itching in uncomfortable situations: then maybe you should repent of your sin. If the scabies of your disease is being picked at and pointed at by mocking onlookers: repent of your sin. If there is a shudder of coming judgment reverberating through your being: repent of your sin. If the cold loneliness of your situation is drawing you at last to the warmth of God's midnight fire: then go to Him and repent of your sin. If you have woken up naked in a pig trough tonight: repent of your sin. If the silence of heaven is making the ears of your own heart twitch and wiggle like a nervous rabbit, yes, if you are living contrary to the commands of Almighty God tonight, AND YOU KNOW IT, then my friend, there is hope! Repent of your sin.

Hyper-grace, especially amongst the present cool and very hip churches of our lands is doing untold damage to both the testimony of the church and the holiness of its members. Let me speak to Christians now: If we regard iniquity in our hearts – then God will not hear any of our prayers except one and that's the one which says "Lord, I am sorry for my sin. I have offended your Holiness, disgraced our family and I am done with it. Right now, I let it go, I leave it off, I put it down, I turn from it to You and ask that You forgive me, and in the place of such cold unrighteousness, You grant me now Your gracious forgiveness, and the warmth of Your felt presence and Your power to live a holy and righteous life. Now Lord, HEAR MY PRAYERS in Jesus name I ask it amen."

Hyper-grace, especially amongst the present cool and very hip churches of our lands is doing untold damage to both the testimony of the church and the holiness of its members.

Here, the called prophet of the covenant people of God gave testimony to the cold hardness of the unheeding ears of the Most High towards His people. Why? Because of their un-repented of sin.

Pastorally I can tell you, that when this same exclusion from the heard favor of the Father is felt by the people of God, then an examination of presently lived in and unconfessed sin is the very first port of call. We can all justify the hard madness of our sin, even coating it in so called 'love'. However, a true curer of souls, and that is what a Pastor must be, a true curer of souls, will open up the wound and go searching for the infection and when finding it will then clear the puss from the soul, even though the sheep might kick and scream! Only a person sick with sin, will need such gnarly shepherds. Unfortunately there are not too many people sick with sin, or gnarly shepherds around nowadays.

So, believe it or not –the hyper-grace movement is now splitting the Evangelical cause. Hyper-grace is manifest in three ways really: 1) In a reinterpretation of the Scriptures; 2) which has led to a laying aside of God's clear teaching of male headship in home and church; 3) which in turn has held to so called 'accepting' Evangelicals where homosexuality is left unjudged and untouched in these churches.

Unfortunately, this arrogant trinity of cowardly selfishness has in turn led to a blind eye being given to a multitude of other 'accepting sins' in the church, ranging from pre-marital sex, to the dating of unbelievers, through to unhindered divorce, and a thousand more sins beside. In emergent and accepting churches, it seems the only sins not tolerated are ecological in nature and those that they deem to halt the promotion of social injustice and humn rights. However, true Evangelicals, that is, Biblical Evangelicals, are not accepting of sin for it is only the repenting of the same which might get God's ears to wiggle once more. FACE IT! If you are a Christian my friend, then you are a 'repenter' and this side of heaven, a regular one at that. Stop accepting that which the Bible calls SIN!

If you are a Christian my friend, then you are a 'repenter' and this side of heaven, a regular one at that. Stop accepting that which the Bible calls SIN

Listen: *For when we were still without strength, in due time Christ died for the ungodly. For scarcely for a righteous man will one die; yet perhaps for a good man someone would even dare to die. But God demonstrates His own love toward us, in that while we were still sinners, Christ died for us. Much more then, having now been justified by His blood, we shall be saved from wrath through Him. Romans 5:6-9 NKJV*

Pray: Turn up the freezer Lord. Make it cold outside Your Kingdom. Make the darkness grip our being and press us tight like the icy pressured depths of the black ocean floor. Open our ears to the howl of the circling wolves and fill us with a drawing fear, that all who are lost would be pulled and pushed to the welcoming orange glow of the courtyard fires of Your midnight love. Have mercy on us O God, have mercy on us before our self made gates surrounding Your fiery indignation are closed forever to those outside. Lord, in Your wrath, remember mercy. Amen and let it be so.

Bible Insight 03

The noon day gropers and other wrestlers in prayer

This is the first question of the prophet. It is a desperate question, for the visions given to Habakkuk were of the utter destruction of his people, and it would appear that though he was the man to 'stand in the gap', there was in fact, no place for him to stand! Regarding his people then, Habakkuk could find no place of repentance. God would not save them from the destruction He was bringing upon them.

Habakkuk 1:2

O Lord, how long shall I cry, And You will not hear? Even cry out to You, "Violence!" And You will not save. NKJV

You see, the old covenant nation had turned aside from the words and commands of the Lord, to go and serve other gods (Deuteronomy 28:14) and now, all the agreed 'cursings' from the dark side of Mount Ebal, which were now racing like a hungry regiment of vengeful and ever hungry *Dinas Vawr's, would come rushing down upon their heads and strip bare the sweet fatness of their sinful valleys.

('The War Song of Dinas Vawr' by Thomas Love Peacock)*

Amidst such typhoon-like wreckage, the beached hulks from the sea of a their sinfulness would sit sentinel, lying embarrassingly to one side, an old high and dry red rust testimony to the terrible repercussion of a broken covenant. And as the felt blackness of their cloud of condemnation covered over the noon day of their skies, even the sighs' of strong interceders, now groping the air in a green coughing fit of mustard spluttered sputum, would bemoan the disconsolate testimony of all the chickens finally coming home to roost.

Question:

"O Lord, how long shall I cry, And You will not hear? Even cry out to You, "Violence!" And You will not save."

Answer:

"And you shall grope at noonday, as a blind man gropes in darkness; you shall not prosper in your ways; you shall be only oppressed and plundered continually, and no one shall save you." Deuteronomy 28:29

There was no saving of these consistent sinful covenant breakers from the bullying brutality of the Chaldean shepherds, no, there was no saving them from the glittering spears of these un-swallowed, red sea Pharaoh-like pursuers of old. The covenant breaker would not see the Chaldeans laid up like so much dead driftwood along the borders of their covenant keeping and protected nation, but rather, like dry timber, the Chaldean judgment wood of God, would now burn upon the alters of all of Judah's false gods, and the spreading flame of God's indignation against them, would leave them as a potash people, strewn along the song bird silent, Auschwitz- like, ash covered ground. Note now, that the narrow ways of God are in fact the broadways of freedom and life. But the broadways of all the sinful and contrary covenant breakers, are the tube narrowed ways of a fast flowing and funneled destruction leading to the hot and ever bubbling Bunsen burner lake of fire.

Maybe now, more than ever, the core message of the Gospel should be unsheathed once more and lain like a slashing sword around the hard hearts of the ungodly?

I wonder, if when our own worried interceders give testimony to finding no solid ground to stand upon and of groping prayers that cannot lay hold of the goodness of God, that it is time to prepare for our own coming typhoon? Maybe now, more than ever, the core message of the Gospel should be unsheathed once more and lain like a slashing sword around the hard hearts of the ungodly?

Listen: *For from you the word of the Lord has sounded forth, not only in Macedonia and Achaia, but also in every place. Your faith toward God has gone out, so that we do not need to say anything. For they themselves declare concerning us what manner of entry we had to you, and how you turned to God from idols to serve the living and true God, and to wait for His Son from heaven, whom He raised from the dead, even Jesus who delivers us from the wrath to come. 1 Thessalonians 1:8-10 NKJV*

Pray: Prepare the mouths of your prophets once more O Lord, and prepare the targets of all their fearless proclamation. Soften hard hearts. Open blind eyes. Send those two ushers of 'fear and trembling' to lead people from the narrow ways of destruction to the wide and open places of that freedom which is found only in Jesus Christ our Lord and Savior. Amen and let it be so.

Bible Insight 04

'Drinking down the damage' or, 'The Habakkuk conundrum'

Violence is that same crime which filled the earth prior to the judgment flood. (Genesis 6:11) and it was the ground upon which God both justified and brought His global cataclysmic judgment.

Habakkuk 1:1,2

The burden which the prophet Habakkuk saw. O Lord, how long shall I cry, And You will not hear? Even cry out to You, "Violence!" And You will not save. NKJV

Habakkuk understands that God abhors such cruel wrongness, such inhuman injustice and undiminishing unruliness, and therefore, he has pounded God's ear with the fact of its rising presence every single day, yes, he has testified to a wobbly and insane society drunk on drinking down damage. So are all the nations who forget God: Drunk with sin. So are all the nations who reject and eject the laws of the Most High: They are drunken nations, pig-like, full of demons, all racing and screaming toward the narrowed edge of a drowning cliff.

Habakkuk was perplexed not only at God's unwilling ears, but at His lack of providing deliverance from such drunken damage. Where was the desert wandering Shepherd when they needed saving from the bullying grabbers of the waters of life? Why had God seemingly gone AWOL? Why is He an absentee landlord? Why is God obviously so uninvolved now in the lives of those He supposedly loves? Habakkuk, you see, is now with boundary broken frustration, angrily knocking on God's door! Yes; with great respect. Yes; with great fearfulness. But in any event, when God's door opens, the prophet himself is going to hand the Most High a summons, demanding He explain Himself!

God will open the door to Habakkuk, however He shall completely ignore the warrant in the prophet's hand, and in the so doing, turn the chattering and chimp-like prophet into a hind, and lead him up to the heights, to witness sights unseen and lay silent his summons and the summons of the ignorant who ask God the wrong questions!

So then dear friends, in our everyday life, what do we do with this 'Habakkuk conundrum,' when God seemingly refuses to act in accordance with His character; when God refuses to save from violence? (And by the way, this of course is the central theme of the prophecy.) Well, we go knocking on God's door. And when He comes to answer us, He shall ignore our misplaced questions and transform us into another animal, taking us on a journey of true seeing and faithful understanding.

Sometimes, often times, God ignores and side steps our questions that He might then take us on a journey, which will in turn, both change our perspective and our very being, forever!

God has no problem with chattering chimps or angry chumps knocking loudly on His door. However, be aware, that God's Theology is often Therianthropic in its effect, and so the next time you look in the mirror, the man you once thought you were might well have disappeared completely!

Sometimes, often times, God ignores and side steps our questions that He might then take us on a journey, which will in turn, both change our perspective and our very being, forever!

Listen: *The Lord God is my strength; He will make my feet like deer's feet, And He will make me walk on my high hills. Habakkuk 3:19 NKJV*

Pray: Lord, please hear our knocking and come to Your door. Lord, please answer our questions and if not, transform and set our feet on the heights of Your land, our land, my land, that I might behold the wonders of the Lord and goodness of God and so be satisfied. Amen and let it be so.

Bible Insight 05

Non-stop through Hairsbreadth

Thus far Habakkuk has essentially asked God "Why don't you answer me?" And then also "Why don't you punish the wicked now?" In the final part of his tri-part question the prophet, in the asking, also accuses God, saying in effect "Why do you allow the continued perversion of Your law by Your lack of intervention?" In other words, "If you are God why don't you do something?" Now then, has there ever been a more up to date question than this one, for I tell you, as a Pastor, I get asked this question many, many times.

Habakkuk 1:3,4

Why do You show me iniquity, And cause me to see trouble? For plundering and violence are before me; There is strife, and contention arises. Therefore the law is powerless, And justice never goes forth. For the wicked surround the righteous; Therefore perverse judgment proceeds. NKJV

Habbakuk is shortly going to understand that God does not always exact immediate judgment, but from the time the station guard blows the whistle of God's conviction, the judgment trains begins to run on two rails of parallel time. 'Lulling' time allows the continuing concrete hardening of hearts. 'Loving' time allows space for contrite spirits to turn in weeping repentance. These two types of time seem to run alongside one another in God's economy , the longer rail curving the direction of the judgment train to one of two destinations of sentencing: The city of 'Hairsbreadth' or the city of 'Destruction'. This train was heading to 'Destruction'.

While we are here, it is of interest to note that one of the indicators of 'Lulling' time is the surrounding of the righteous by the wicked such that all the products of politics are perversity. That is, there is a specific surrounding, a purposed enclosing and a bitter besieging of the righteous for the purpose of a strangulating overrunning. Look now at the politicians and their financial backers, who have 'Salami sliced' their way to the core of our once imperfect but Biblical related pillars of society!

Like runaway cancer, they have corrupted the lungs of our nation, bent double the upright, infected the brains of the ignorant and rotted the genitals of righteous reproduction. The city of 'Hairsbreadth' has passed us by dear friends, and there is no health left in us and the bend in the track is coming to an end.

We must now prepare for a very different world of brutal unrighteousness to so speedily but temporarily come upon us. Are you prepared for this

We must now prepare for a very different world of brutal unrighteousness to so speedily but temporarily come upon us. Are you prepared for this?

I see 'Destruction' in the distance.

Listen: *The Lord God is my strength; He will make my feet like deer's feet, And He will make me walk on my high hills. Habakkuk 3:19 NKJV*

Pray: Lord, Your 'Lulling' time is coming to an end and all that is left is hardness of heart and the long shadow of a sign that says, 'Work makes one free.' Oh twist us back to the city of 'Hairsbreadth' and have mercy on us once more, O Lord our God and King. Amen and let it be so.

Bible Insight 06

Eagles Eerie and the 'Habakkuk Hatch'

I used to live in Chingford Hatch, a 'Hatch,' being an old English word to describe a clear and open place of passing, in a densely wooded area.

Habakkuk 1:4

Therefore the law is powerless, And justice never goes forth. For the wicked surround the righteous; Therefore perverse judgment proceeds. NKJV

The law of God is holy and just and good, but unless it is honored, obeyed and enacted, it is impotent, yes, unless the law becomes the main ingredient in the mix of society, it simply becomes an impotent bystander in the affairs of men and is become irrelevant. Such is the law of God at the beginning of the 21st century.

In the West and in the USA in particular, great has been the wailing at the removal of those tablets of stone containing those ten wonderful laws. The real truth, however, is that those ten commands which once undergirded the constitution, written and otherwise of former Christian nations of the world, have, by wicked men and women, long since been 'Salami sliced' out of all forms of earthly justice. So much so, that the law of God has been made so ineffective and powerless that its child of justice has had its legs publicly amputated at the hip, and cruelly severed at the thigh.

Our lands and are immediate futures are now being shaped by man-made laws, and rotted by the cultural expedients of all things sinfully human, of all things anti-God and all things anti-Christ. The claws of incorrectness are now the midnight gouging we hear outside the doors of the last bastions of God laws, and the weeping, well, the weeping is the ancient ghost of 'Lot' that old spirit of compromise and convenience, which has been conjured up among us in the church by them that know not God; those money grabbing, horn-rimmed hipsters and cool touters of old heresies, who for so long now have taken that spirit of Lot and masqueraded him as 'love' and 'live and let live', whilst at the same time, turning out those three sentinels of sanity: 'absolute, truth and judgment' and forcing them from the high lands of love, to go and pollute themselves in the lowlands of leprosy.

We make the law effectively powerful once more, yes, we turn the law of God into the leaven of a society gone bad and raise it back to its once so healthy height by again living by the law of God! Can we do this where we live? It will be virtually impossible. Can we go somewhere else to do this? No, for there are no new lands left upon this globe to run to anymore, and there are no more vacant hills for the building of a new Jerusalem here on earth. So then, I propose we have but three options.

Where peaceful and present legitimate means become impossible, yes, where freedom of speech and exclusion from the market place of politics, education and religion become the nasty norm, then our second option is to resist, it is to revolt!

The first is by all legal and legitimate means, to boldly proclaim and brazenly practice that which the Word of God teaches. So, where we can, within our own systems of political 'allowability', let us with all sincerity, be the people of God and by the grace of God, seek to recover the hearts, minds and practices of societies gone so Biblically wrong. For this to happen, the pulpits and all the institutional platforms of proclamation must be bought back (there will be a great price to pay here), then the wells need to be cleared out, and their mouths opened up once more to become the silver-tongued springs of solid Biblical declaration.

Where peaceful and present legitimate means become impossible, yes, where freedom of speech and exclusion from the market place of politics, education and religion become the nasty norm, then our second option is to resist, it is to revolt! It is to partition the land; it is to draw the battle lines; it is to engage in division. Two thousand years of church history has shown that for the Christian, such resistance toward division is ever a personal choice and it is usually a choice forced upon them by bloody persecution. The measure of such resistance to division and its success will be dictated by quantity of men, money, munitions in all its varied forms that are available. Are we ready for such a revolution? Do we have all that we can to so succeed? Should we as Christians even try this?

The third option we have is the 'Habakkuk Hatch' that is, we need to see what's coming, we need to see the walk of Birnam wood and then wait for

And there will be blood; their blood, and rivers of it.

the clearing to appear, the space, the place of 'Habakkuk's Hatch' and there get on our knees and watch and pray. For if what is about to come upon our nation is the direct judgment of God upon a hard-necked people who have made His revealed and holy law so socially impotent, then all resistance is futile! That yardstick of the laid aside law will now so frighteningly become the terrible measurement of the depth of judgment about to over flow us.

As I write, these three options are still before us, only just maybe, but there are still these three. Should we ever move to option two of 'resistance to division,' then God will have to somehow disarm the powerful godless governments which will come against us. Without this happening, the slaughter which will follow will make the Huguenot horror look like a picnic.

Therefore, it seems to me, that option three is maybe the only option we shall see. Let us then take our nimble feet to the high places of observation and in faith, through the coming desolation, in that space of grace provided for us amongst the war-like trees, see the sword of the wicked eventually turned upon themselves.

Now then, should this ever not happen, then please be assured of this: that the great and on- going gathering of 'the wood wicked' is simply fuel for the fire and tables for the purpose of 'abattoirial' slaughter. And there will be blood; their blood, and rivers of it. Those two tablets of the present powerless laws of God, their fleshless and unspeaking jaws lying bleached white in the sand above this godless sky, shall soon be taken up by the coming Samson-Jesus, who with uncut hair and rampant eye, shall smite them dead with hip and thigh.

I am living in 'Habakkuk's Hatch'. I will not cower to godless power. As for you, which of these three options will you be choosing today?

Listen: *Now Enoch, the seventh from Adam, prophesied about these men also, saying, "Behold, the Lord comes with ten thousands of His saints, to execute judgment on all, to convict all who are ungodly among them of all their ungodly deeds which they have committed in an ungodly way, and of all the harsh things which ungodly sinners have spoken against Him." Jude 14-15 NKJV*

Pray: Lord, we have no power to resist. If we had, then so we would and so we should. But Lord, this host is in Your hand! So, have mercy upon us Your people and help us stand in the Hatch, in the space between the weeping and proclaim Your present judgment and that only safety that is in the spear-pierced side of Your Son Jesus. Take us to Your Eagle's Eerie Lord today, and shelter us in Etam, even in the cleft of the rock. Amen and let it be so.

Bible Insight 07

Do not cower to perverted power

So here in Habakkuk, the strangling and setting aside of God's law has not, I say, has not removed the nations legal system. It has simply replaced it and replaced it with perverted laws, leading to a body of replacement law which is essentially there to shore up that system of God rejection, which is now become the system of the selfishness of the current elite, whoever they may be, in whatever political framework they manifest themselves in, even from communism to fascism and every shade in between and beyond. When God's law is rejected perverse judgments proceed: The removal of a death penalty for capital crimes; the legalization of murder in the form of abortion; the legalization of gay marriage and a thousand more besides, are all perversions, bent arrows full of self-cursing which will always miss God's mark. Christians cannot obey such legal perversion in any form and must stop cowering to perverted power. In such cases of continued perversion, civil obedience becomes public affirmation of sin. Tell me, how can Christians give approval to perversion?

Habakkuk 1:4

Therefore the law is powerless, And justice never goes forth. For the wicked surround the righteous; Therefore perverse judgment proceeds. NKJV

In the face of such perversion, I am not only approving of civil disobedience, I am commending it and recommending it. The Christian cowering to present perverted power must stop. Using all Biblically legitimate means, as individuals, we must personally stand against the going forth of godlessness even if our neck becomes hurt with the turning, and our cheeks red with the slapping, yes, even when our feet pulse with the pain of yet another extra mile and our coatless back is wet with the cold dew of another morning without a roof.

Now then, when we then unite and organize 'illegal' civil disobedience, reminding ourselves that in standing against perversion we shall break their godless laws, I say their laws and not God's laws, then such a so-called 'illegal' unity of resistance becomes a threat to present perversion and shall be attacked by them and in the attacking, their opening slander may eventually lead even to slaughter. I ask again then, "Should the Christian then be prepared for armed conflict with his or her own government?"

There is only one arm that the Christian can Biblically introduce into such situations and that is 'the arm of the Lord' and the 'arm of the Lord' is none other than Jesus Himself. Jesus is the extension of God into all of our troubles and He is become our only shield and sword, and this outstretched arm of God in the flesh, shall truly save us from the slavery of all perversions. So, in our 'illegal' civil disobedience, we must trust Jesus to save us and fight for us. Be aware right now that to introduce any other arms of flesh into such a sad situation will lead to destruction, and you shall have on your hands anything from what shall be regarded by the perverts as guerilla-terrorist cells to civil war. 9mm, you see, may be just enough in distance travelled to turn a nation to civil war. Be careful now. Be very careful.

Governments must realize that legal authority does necessarily correlate with righteous rule and the continued rulings of blind unrighteousness will lead to eventual unruliness in a disenfranchised people. As a parent of society then, elected or otherwise, Governments must not provoke their children to wrath.

Governments must realize that legal authority does necessarily correlate with righteous rule and the continued rulings of blind unrighteousness will lead to eventual unruliness in a disenfranchised people. As a parent of society then, elected or otherwise, Governments must not provoke their children to wrath.

Here in Habakkuk, God is now rolling up His sleeves and baring His arms, for God's answer to the perversion of His holy law in Israel is the Chaldeans. Here they come now! Here they come.

As for you dear reader, look around you now. What might be God's answer in your own nation of perversion?

Listen: *If it is possible, as much as depends on you, live peaceably with all men. Beloved, do not avenge yourselves, but rather give place to wrath; for it is written, "Vengeance is Mine, I will repay," says the Lord. Therefore "If your enemy is hungry, feed him; If he is thirsty,*

give him a drink; For in so doing you will heap coals of fire on his head." Do not be overcome by evil, but overcome evil with good.
Romans 12:18-21NKJV

Pray: Father, we shall be subject to governing authority, but not sin and not to unrighteousness and not to evil. When we find ourselves in such unhappy tension, teach us to pray and then will You come and take vengeance upon our hateful enemies. Amen and let it be so.

Bible Insight 08

The smelly outcome of incontinent cats cooked in a dead dog pie

T he decades old, two meter high, Titan Arum, or 'Corpse plant' is an inflorescent, that is a plant consisting of hundreds of small flowers flourishing from a single proud stem, whose foul odor attracts the carrion insects and flesh flies to its putrid pollination party.

Habakkuk 1:5

They are terrible and dreadful; Their judgment and their dignity proceed from themselves. NKJV

Anarchists may have no dignity, yet despite their nomenclature, they do have laws, yes, they do have some measurement of judgment, be it ever so base, so as not to utterly consume themselves.

Here in our text for tonight, we see that the consuming jaws of this judgment visitation people which would eat up the chosen of God and then swallow the other nations of the then known world, not only had laws, but along with them, had a proclaimed and projected, self-styled excellence of lawful application, which, in turn, then produced a great deluded dignity of a strong self-standing and a solid self-centered nationhood. However, this conquering cabal, judged themselves by themselves, and consequently, all their laws and that dignity and excellence of their national pride encased therein, proceeded solely from themselves. Such self judgment, and such self-measured personal and national pride is however, a thorn surrounded titanic Corpse flower, whose root reaches deep into the ground of pride and whose bed is fertilized with a pit-foul arrogance, the collective and conceited stench of which, is like the used anal wipes of a Crete public toilet on a hot summers day afternoon. So are all the nations who now forsake the Lord and His laws. So is America; so is Britain; and so is Europe.

Now then, in the nations which have forsaken the Lord and His laws; yes, in the nations who have now long ejected the Bible from their beds and from the backyards of their now unholy habitations, the 'Necrophilia Americana' have come to lay their larvae in all those old and cancerous Kentucky lungs, who smoked themselves to breathless loss whilst murdering their own babies and dropping bombs on those other mothers they considered 'badder then themselves'. 'Pride cometh before a fall,' and the present exaltation of the law firm of 'Simon Fitzpatrick and Patrick Fitzsimon' will simply further call the flesh flies to the feast of the now bent body of a dying country, consumed by self judgment and self indulgence, and clothed in the heavy, heavy back-bending cloak of a thoroughly sodden and urine soaked pride. Do you see this now? Do you see the nation which has forsaken the Lord?

Whilst checking your own armpits for any foul smell of pride, be sure to wash yourselves daily with the Word of God. The rest leave. Don't even let the smell of them be found on your clothing. Get out of the way and get yourselves ready. God is coming.

> *'Simon Fitzpatrick and Patrick Fitzsimon' will simply further call the flesh flies to the feast of the now bent body of a dying country, consumed by self-judgment and self indulgence, and clothed in the heavy, heavy back-bending cloak of a thoroughly sodden and urine soaked pride*

Listen: *Behold, the day of the Lord comes, Cruel, with both wrath and fierce anger, To lay the land desolate; And He will destroy its sinners from it. For the stars of heaven and their constellations Will not give their light; The sun will be darkened in its going forth, And the moon will not cause its light to shine. "I will punish the world for its evil, And the wicked for their iniquity; I will halt the arrogance of the proud, And will lay low the haughtiness of the terrible. I will make a mortal more rare than fine gold, A man more than the golden wedge of Ophir. Therefore I will shake the heavens, And the earth will move out of her place, In the wrath of the Lord of hosts And in the day of His fierce anger. It shall be as the hunted gazelle, And as a sheep that no man takes up; Every man will turn to his own people, And everyone will flee to his own land. Everyone who is found will be thrust through, And everyone who is captured will fall by the sword. Their children also will be dashed to pieces before their eyes; Their houses will be plundered And their wives ravished. "Behold, I will stir up the Medes against them, Who will not regard silver; And as for gold, they will not delight in it. Also their bows will dash the young men to pieces, And they will have no pity on the fruit of the womb; Their eye will not spare children. And Babylon, the glory of kingdoms, The beauty of the Chaldeans' pride, Will be as when God overthrew Sodom and Gomorrah. Isaiah 13:9-19 NKJV*

Pray: Father, we humble ourselves before You. We have forsaken Your laws, denied Your grace, abused Your goodness, abandoned Your ways. Have mercy on us O Lord, and if You will, in Your anger, remember mercy. Amen and let it be so.

Bible Insight 09

The Borg of the Lord

There now follows five verses describing the sword of God's judgment, the Chaldeans. They are bitter and hasty, terrible and dreadful, filled with unrelenting violence and overflowing with scoffing derision, they are hungry devourers and merciless enslavers, fuelled by such a self-love, that regarding every obstacle, they simply 'adapt and overcome.' To such an all consuming, hungry and carnivorous swarm, any national resistance was futile. Now then, I have purposely quoted Habakkuk 1:6 from the KJV tonight, as the opening statement is more pronounced in this translation. "LOOK!" say's God, "Lo, I raise up the Chaldeans."

Habakkuk 1:6

For, lo, I raise up the Chaldeans, that bitter and hasty nation, which shall march through the breadth of the land, to possess the dwelling places that are not theirs. KJV

Here then, God shall use a godless and unrighteous nation to judge His wayward covenanting people. Indeed, God Himself has raised up and shaped this sharp threshing sledge for such a time as this. Mark well then today, that on planet earth, behind the black gates of Mordor it is not Sauron who is building an army of Orcs beneath Mount doom, no, it is God! "Lo, I raise up the Chaldeans."

How then can we know when it is darkness and the devil and an infestation of the demonic which raises up a wicked nation against us and even a confederation of nations to come against the righteous light seekers, the holy light holders and the freedom from sin proclaimers? I say again: how can we know when the originator of destruction is God or the devil? Well, there is an easy answer to this question. When a nation is indeed a seeker of light and a holder of righteousness and a proclaimer of the same, then God will never come against it. Ever! Any adversity against such a nation finds its sources solely in the devil. However, when a nation sniffs at holiness, when a nation snuffs out righteousness and when a nation calls bad 'good' and darkness 'light', then I tell you, it is

God who is driving calamity like a stampeding herd of ten thousand rampaging cattle, right down the main streets of every city of that now light rejecting nation. Resistance is futile. "Lo, I raise up the Chaldeans."

Behind which black gate on earth is God now raising up a new locust swarm of nation consuming judgment?

Look around you now Christian, look at the movement of nations. Look around you now, look at the rise and fall of walls, look at the opening and closing of gates, look at the spread of the dark eagle's wings! Behind which black gate on earth is God now raising up a new locust swarm of nation consuming judgment?

Be sure of this: that God is at work among the nations and toward some of them, He is sharpening a sword of judgment, especially against those other 'dimmer switch' nations who have so shamelessly rejected His light and, then, like a used cigarette butt, has screw-heeled His grace into the baby blood leached ground.

Listen: *For, lo, I raise up the Chaldeans, that bitter and hasty nation, which shall march through the breadth of the land, to possess the dwelling places that are not theirs. Habakkuk 1:6 KJV*

Pray: Sovereign Lord, God over all, who should not be in awe of You? Merciful and patient, loving and gracious, creator of time and all the built spaces for repentance therein, the wind now carries to us the sound of the sharpening of Your sword of judgment. In Your wrath, remember mercy, and look upon the quick ignorance of we 'forgeters of God' we 'forsakers of grace' and soften our hearts that we might receive Your correction and be saved. Amen and let it be so.

Bible Insight 10

Terms of lease

Habakkuk 1:6

For indeed I am raising up the Chaldeans, A bitter and hasty nation Which marches through the breadth of the earth, To possess dwelling places that are not theirs. NKJV

The people of this planet have been involved in warring with one another ever since Cain killed Able. Since time immemorial we have had: Envy Wars; Hate Wars; Succession Wars; Civil Wars; Independence Wars; Ethnic Cleansing Wars; Religious Wars; Political Wars; Guerilla Wars, Terrorist Wars and Resource Wars; and no doubt you could add a few more to my list. In the coming years, we shall no doubt see more of the same of these types of war appear across the globe, however, I suspect it will be the terrible trio of the political war, the religious war and especially the resource war which will kill the most people. Indeed, as the world's population increases, together with the demand for its dwindling resources, then it is the resource war which shall initially make demands of the acquisition of those lands, under long and historical dispute over ownership, and further, under various pretense, might even arrange an opportunity for invasion and the possession that 'which is not theirs'. Now then, is such 'stealing' sin?

"The earth is the Lord's and the fullness thereof," and thus far He has only officially portioned one small segment of this fullness of geography and associated resources to the people of Israel. If then resource theft is sin, then stealing from God is plain stupidity for 'the strong man armed, always keeps his goods in peace'. The nations must leave Israel and her resources alone, lest we find that it is God almighty that turns around and lays hold of our pick-pocket dipping wrist. Only trouble can follow such an Almighty apprehension.

The coming further resource wars involve the forced acquisition of dwelling places belonging to another, and consequently, legally speaking, together with its resource content, all the earth space surrounding such stolen dwelling places, whether these resources be below them under the ground, even right down to the very centre of the earth, and then even the air space above them. Such 'theft invasion', to various degrees, not only dispossesses the original owners but disperses them or subjugates them, or eventually, absorbs or eradicates them.

The safety of any physical dwelling place therefore is at the behest of God, not stealth delivery

"The earth is the Lord's and the fullness thereof." Therefore, all devil run democracies, (oh wake up now!) and all other political, social, economic and cultural entities, exist and promulgate themselves on a planet which does not belong to them. Therefore, the possession of any land mass with its associate resources are all ultimately held leasehold and therefore temporarily, at the discretion of the one true landlord, that is, the Lord God Almighty!

"The earth is the Lord's and the fullness thereof," so listen up now. Throughout time, though the devil has had his Kingdom's overlaying the surface of this spinning orb, 'the earth is STILL the Lord's and the fullness thereof.' Do you see that? The kingdoms of this world may belong to the devil, but all the substance and solid nature of planet earth belongs to God and so does the disposing of the same. "I am raising up the Chaldeans, ...to possess dwelling places that are not theirs." In other words, God is rightly leasing to them, this oh so nasty nation, both place and property which is not theirs. God and God alone has the right to do this and when He does, the transaction and transfer is unstoppable.

The safety of any physical dwelling place therefore is at the behest of God, not stealth delivery weapons, or arms both nuclear and nasty. The disposal of other people's dwelling places into our lap is also at the behest of God and when this happens, it might just involve another war, a God war. The possession of the promised land was a 'God War', and resulted in the unstoppable total transfer of land property and possession of the same. So let us ask ourselves, outside of that particular time and incident, has there been any other 'God War'? The answer of course is yes. Look now, "I am raising up the Chaldeans, ...to possess dwelling places that are not theirs." Think about this: When a renter 'reallocates' an owners resources it is theft. When the owner reallocates his resources, then it is his both his desire and right. "The earth is the Lord's and the fullness thereof."

How can we discern between the wicked actions of the devil's burglars stealing resources which are not theirs and the 'legal' actions of God's bailiffs? Especially, how can we know when a 'God War' is being pursued against us? Well, remember, when a landlord's property is being destroyed, when a landlord's place is being utilized for actions contrary to the owners original declared intent, yes, when the owners name is being brought into open disrepute and when proper payment and right honor is long overdue, then we should not be surprised when a removals van pulls up outside our house and some burly men start banging on our door. Should our nations expect a visit from God's bailiffs?

Tell me now then: "Have our nations been served and eviction notice?"

Habakkuk is later going to see the rightness of this kind of 'God War' eviction. However, Habakkuk is also going to have big problems with God's bailiffs, the Chaldeans. Yes, Habakkuk shall have problems in understanding the kind of 'eviction people' that God uses to reclaim His property. We shall look at this later, but for tonight, know that although God uses some brutal bailiffs to evict His bad tenants, once the task is completed, the bad bailiffs themselves will also be dealt with. There is nothing nice about God's redistribution of resource.

Tonight then, know three things:

"The earth is the Lord's and the fullness thereof." He distributes it as He pleases.

The safety of any dwelling place and its continuance is at the behest of the owner. Only God can make us dwell in the safety of possession, provision and peace.

God is in the eviction game even today.

Tell me now then: "Have our nations been served and eviction notice?"

Listen: *The earth is the Lord's, and all its fullness, The world and those who dwell therein. For He has founded it upon the seas, And established it upon the waters. Who may ascend into the hill of the Lord? Or who may stand in His holy place? He who has clean hands and a pure heart, Who has not lifted up his soul to an idol, Nor sworn* *deceitfully. He shall receive blessing from the Lord, And righteousness from the God of his salvation. This is Jacob, the generation of those who seek Him, Who seek Your face. Selah Psalms 24:1-6 NKJV*

Pray: Sovereign Father, when our nations lay under You, God most high, then we can truly lay ourselves down and sleep in peace, dwelling in Your gracious safety. But You Lord are known by the judgment You execute and the wicked shall indeed be snared in the work of his own hands and turned into hell. So shall all the nations that forget God. Remember Lord please, that in the nations of the willful sinful, there are still those few who have not forgotten You O God. Have mercy then O Lord, and turn us once again to You. Amen and let it be so.

Bible Insight 11

An Haiku of national decapitation

So today, God now begins His five verse description of His sword of national judgment. Here is a nation who measures itself by itself. Here is a nation whose standards and laws proceed from their own pragmatic and self-serving decisions. True justice and right judgment however come only from the law of the Lord.

Habakkuk 1:7

They are terrible and dreadful; Their judgment and their dignity proceed from themselves. NKJV

The continuing eradication of the Ten Commandments presence from any culture, will ultimately lead to the utter selfishness of an all-consuming hedonistic and homosexual madness (Genesis 18:19,20). I say ultimately, because there are many stages to this self-consuming cancer. So for now, in the case of the Chaldeans, such national self-judgment has led to dignity of self-elevation that can only be measured by a few millimeters, you know, just like you would see the rising of a puss bound scab standing raised and craggy just above the skin of an infected pauper, even a poor and pitiful, disease-ridden leper. So is the self-made dignity of any nation which has rejected the law of the Lord and whose judgment and justice now proceed totally from themselves. Such a leprous legion may have their bright flag unfurled and a fluttering; yes, their chest may be puffed out and bedecked full of rainbow colored medals, but God calls such a nations self-made dignity leprous, scabby, disgusting and unclean in His sight.

The rejection of God's laws always eventually leads to cultural pragmatism that screams through the streets of time like a doped up druggy on an overdose of 'speed'. Such are such unholy nations who make their laws up as they go along to justify and further enable their own self-consuming ways. Their will is their law. So when such a nation marches forth to war, they are fearfully frightful, yes, they cause the observer, the source of their current consuming, to cringe and hide in heart-collapsing fear. Why is this? because nations which make up their own laws can justify genocide and murder millions to achieve their ends.

Such nations can put a brutal boot up anyone's behind to move them along, kick them out of the way and grind them into the ground.

The last 100 years of European history has not seen the coming and going of many wars, even two world wars, but rather, has experienced the nation-consuming ravages of many battles in but one major war: the war to eventually in any, and in every way, overturn the law of God and even eradicate it from the earth to make way for one human world government and one ultimate anti-God ruler. Now even today, the nations of the world are thoroughly rejecting the law of the Lord and make no mistake about it, those of us who carry it in our hearts and live it in our lives, will be silenced by them, shut up, eradicated. Nations without God, show no grace or mercy toward those who know the Lord and His law.

A sharp crescent sword waits to take the selfish head and shout 'God is great'.

Look America, piece by piece, from education, legislation, politics and public place, your Judeo-Christian foundation stones are being now most hastily removed.

Look Great Britain, your empire and Nation is left to you foundationless and desolate.

Look Europe, the past pride of your nations are being ground into a powder keg of mixed populations whilst your skylines are full of banks and minarets, and the aroma of the late evening air is full of foreboding, even while the pilfering politicians talk of peace and bathe in plenty.

A sharp crescent sword waits to take the selfish head and shout 'God is great'.

Listen: *The wicked shall be turned into hell, And all the nations that forget God. For the needy shall not always be forgotten; The expectation of the poor shall not perish forever. Psalms 9:17-18 NKJV*

Pray: "Restore us, O God of our salvation, and cause Your anger toward us to cease. Will You be angry with us forever? Will You prolong Your anger to all generations? Will You not revive us again, that Your people may rejoice in You? Show us Your mercy, Lord, and grant us Your salvation. I will hear what God the Lord will speak, for He will speak peace to His people and to His saints; But let them not turn back to folly. Surely His salvation is near to those who fear Him, that glory may dwell in our land. (Psalms 85:4-9) NKJV

Bible Insight 12

Habakkuk's Haboob and how to keep the evening wolves at bay

Habakkuk hoped for sounds of revival across the tops of his mulberry trees, instead, all he hears is the unsheathing of sharp metal. Now, God gives Habakkuk not an unpacked explanation of His doings, but a continued revelation of His sovereignty among the nations beginning with a stinging paper-cutting description of this scything sword of judgment: The Chaldeans, that coming soon, all-consuming, totally infiltrating, devastating desert storm. It is as if God now raises a black Haboob in the mind of His prophet and within its falling wall of enveloping sand, forms animalistic pictures of all-consuming horror for him to take a most thorough note of.

Habakkuk 1:8

Their horses also are swifter than leopards, And more fierce than evening wolves. NKJV

The first of these is the Leopard, those Lion-Panthers, head heavy with comparatively massive skulls compared to their body size, those Pit bulls of the cat kingdom, those nocturnal stealth machines, which can crunch their way through any beast, eating anything and consuming everything they catch, and with a top speed of up to 57kmph, these light footed leopards, look as though they fly with open jaws upon their unsuspecting prey, suddenly appearing 'as if out of nowhere'. Be sure dear friends that the devil can also appear in your day 'as if out of nowhere'. Do not be surprised at his appearing therefore, but rather, be ready!

The snorting transport of the Chaldeans are just as swift as these seeming dimension jumping killing machines, and so, being built for battle, these hungry hunter mounts, are now described as appearing even more ravenous and voracious, more angry and desperately daring, than those hungry evening wolves which are infuriated by a day of passing hunger. Make no mistake about it, the evening wolves in their fantastic fury will so devour you, that in the morning, not even a bone shall be left

(Zephaniah 3:3). One of the reasons 'Night Whispers' exists, is to warn you dear reader about the terror of these evening wolves. At evening, the devil is prepared more than ever to come and take you and rip you apart. Therefore allow me today to warn you of the same.

The coming of night for the fighting Christian is a time of comparative weakness. The spent day has consumed all our resistive resources. The devil has been defeated, victory has adorned our way, our shield has been held high, our sword has been quick to slay, but now the day departs and darkness draweth nigh,

When the night time Haboob covers the good works of our day, let us watch out for the evening wolves that inhabit the way to our nightly rest. For you Christian, there is no greater time of danger than the evening of the well fought day.

and it is time for the renewal of food and rest, yes, it is time to retreat to our own city, to the fold of the Great Shepherd and the sleep of the just. This way, this time, this quiet walk back to the true home of our hearts, is punctuated by the howl of the evening wolves. Regret; Self-deceiving; Self-deserving; Self-loathing; Loneliness; Unwarranted dread; Worry; Care; Doubt; Disappointment; Betrayal; Anger; False teaching; Oppression; Possession, Legion and Lying words; are all just a few names of the salivating monsters howling among this large devil's evening wolf pack, and be sure of this, that at the end of your victorious day, they are following you into the sheep fold, ever ready to consume you. Be prepared to protect yourself.

In the evening, we still protect ourselves, by letting the memory of the sacrifice of Christ be upon us in the evening hours. So then, let His bread be in our mouth and His sweet wine upon our lips. Let the word of Christ dwell in us richly, and let the song of His praise be on our lips, the cup of thankfulness in our left hand and the sword of the Spirit in our right. God is good. Let us declare it: "God is good!" And during our sleeping hours He is awake and works on our behalf to bring goodness to our feet in the dawn of the morning. So shall we, despite the outer howling, lay ourselves down to peace sleep and dwell in His most particular safety.

When the night time Haboob covers the good works of our day, let us watch out for the evening wolves that inhabit the way to our nightly rest. For you Christian, there is no greater time of danger than the evening of the well fought day. Let this Psalm of David be on your lips tonight:

Listen: *O God, You are my God; Early will I seek You; My soul thirsts for You; My flesh longs for You In a dry and thirsty land Where there is no water. So I have looked for You in the sanctuary, To see Your power and Your glory. Because Your lovingkindness is better than life, My lips shall praise You. Thus I will bless You while I live; I will lift up my hands in Your name. My soul shall be satisfied as with marrow and fatness, And my mouth shall praise You with joyful lips. When I remember You on my bed, I meditate on You in the night watches. Because You have been my help, Therefore in the shadow of Your wings I will rejoice. My soul follows close behind You; Your right hand upholds me. NKJV*

Pray: Oh my God, hear me when I whisper to you this evening. O God of my righteousness: you have made space for me today when I have been in distress. In defeat you have been gracious and in victory I have praised you. Now, as the evening shadows lengthen, have mercy upon me, and hear my prayer. LORD you have set apart the godly for yourself and so You will hear when I call to You. I am still standing in awe. I am wholly in You, indeed, I am holy in You. My heart is still and I testify to myself and to heaven, that I trust in You. Be good to me this evening then, and in the darkness, let the night-light of Your gracious countenance be around me heart and mind. According to Your will, the morning comes for me great God, and with it, the strengthening of Your breath, and clothed in Your goodness. So, tonight I shall rest as Your tomorrow shall be prepared for me, yet another victorious day to know You. Amen and let it be so.

Bible Insight 13

Habakkuk's hyperphaigiac hunters

There are three things to note then regarding these lion-panther-wolves:

First, is that this cavalry is widespread, (their chargers charge ahead), that is they are all encompassing and proudly pressing on, racing each other to their prey. There is no angle from which they shall not come; there is no place on the compass from which they shall not strike. They are widespread.

Habakkuk 1:8

Their horses also are swifter than leopards, And more fierce than evening wolves. Their chargers charge ahead; Their cavalry comes from afar; They fly as the eagle that hastens to eat. NKJV

Second, is that they are untiring. Yes indeed, they may have a long distance to travel to come to the cities of Judah, even to the capital Jerusalem, but no matter, they are untiring, un-resting and ever voracious in their driving and vicious intent. They 'come on'. They 'come on' some more, and then they 'come on' again. Remember, at the end of the round, you may be exhausted and sat on your stool in your corner, gulping in water and being fanned by your second whilst instructed by your coach, but the unrelenting opponent is still on their feet, skipping around and staring you down, shadow boxing and waiting for the bell to ring once more. Like these Chaldeans, they are as fresh as morning daisies and as pretty and primed as a Venus Fly Trap.

Thirdly, they are ravenous. They do not come to fight, they come to eat. They come to indulge their excessive and extreme appetite. You see, the battle outcome is not in question here, just the time of dinner.

So then, these mounted bowmen, these spear carrying lancers, were allowed to come upon the covenant nation because the people of God had broken the covenant and now the curse their fathers agreed to were about to be beaten around their pitiful self-enhancing hearts and their proud ,

proud heads. There was national sin in Israel and national sin led to national judgment.

We may feel safe in our islands, even in our continent separated from the rest of the world by vast sweeps of water. We may feel safe in our technology, yes, our rockets may form an iron dome above us, our missiles a metal wall before us, and our ICBM's like a bolero hammer, trigger ready to crush the heads of any oncoming 'numpties' foolish enough to try to take us out or take us over. No matter. I say, no matter, for when God, with vengeance in His heart, moves out of a nation's way, then the great unseen sea wall of protection is removed and swiftly, like a high tided and angry sea, yes, like a concrete toppling Tsunami, a volcano in the East can devastate and overrun all the inlands of the West.

We are not Israel. But we are a nation once blessed by God, once under God, once proud to call the LORD our God. Now, we are not Israel. But they are a nation which forgot God and so are we. Look what happened to them

We are not Israel. But we are a nation once blessed by God, once under God, once proud to call the LORD our God. Now, we are not Israel. But they are a nation which forgot God and so are we. Look what happened to them.

Fear of judgment has not pushed our nations back toward the Lord. Financial disaster has not pushed our nations back to God. Tower toppling terrorism has not pushed our nation back to God. Disease and the terrible dismemberment of our soldiers, blown to pieces on foreign battle fields has not pushed our nation back to God. The collapse of all things we counted as precious: marriage; family; babies, has not pushed our nations back to God. Neither has the rise of any social monstrosity pushed us back to God. No, in the sight of all these things, the church of the living God is still singing love songs whilst handing out sick bags to drunks on a Saturday night. Consequently, our nation has not been called back to God and neither has it any intention to be called back.

In my dreams, I hear hoof beats. And in the day, I feel the pounding of the ground. Judgment is coming. Are you ready?

Listen: *The Lord will bring a nation against you from afar, from the end of the earth, as swift as the eagle flies, a nation whose language you* *will not understand, a nation of fierce countenance, which does not respect the elderly nor show favor to the young. And they shall eat the increase of your livestock and the produce of your land, until you are destroyed; they shall not leave you grain or new wine or oil, or the increase of your cattle or the offspring of your flocks, until they have destroyed you. Deuteronomy 28:49-51 NKJV*

Pray: Father, whatever it takes, turn our hearts to You once more. Amen and let it be so.

Bible Insight 14

Thugs, thieves and aggregate dealers

The terrible description of the Chaldean cavalry continues apace. These eagle swift and voracious, unrelenting, lion-panther wolves are pitiless. They do not come to parley, they come to do violence. No crying will stop them. No negotiation can defer them. Indeed, neither the defenselessness of youth nor the silver-haired sage shall suffer them to show any kindness or respect. They are come for violence. They are come for possession. They are uncaring thugs. They are happy thieves. They are people takers. They are slave makers. Like the wide-mouthed East wind comes and sups up the sand, shipping it to distant lands and piling it up in heaps, so the Chaldeans like aggressive aggregate dealers shall gather up peoples and ship them into servitude, their captive nets, bristling and full, like the baleen of the bowhead whale as they plunge into the swarms of plankton-scampering people trying to flee from them, running across the face of the earth.

Habakkuk 1:9

"They all come for violence; Their faces are set like the east wind. They gather captives like sand. NKJV

The devil would either have you dead or have you in his service. How he kills you, or how he enslaves you is of no consequence to him. The devil is a violent murderer and a thief. The devil is a thuggish slave owner and a dealer in flesh. The devil is not our nation's friend, and the freedoms he pushes, for now, are simply but golden manacles and furry handcuffs. Just as Heroin always has its hook and 'Crack' its' crazy killing consummation, so all the drug pushed politically correct laws shall also enslave the generations in weakness and collapse.

Whatever the cost, now is the time to stand up to the drug pushing political correctness of the great enemy of our souls, that long lived liar, that ever noisy accuser of the brethren, that blatant blasphemer, that killer of humanity, that ancient murderer, the devil. Now is the time to stand up.

Listen: *Therefore take up the whole armor of God, that you may be able to withstand in the evil day, and having done all, to stand. Stand* *therefore, having girded your waist with truth, having put on the breastplate of righteousness. Ephesians 6:13-14NKJV*

Pray: Lord, make my tongue like a sharp sword and my chest like solid iron. Father, glorify Yourself in me today no matter what the cost. Amen and let it be so.

Bible Insight 15

The three attorneys of the flesh: 'Scoff, Scorn and Derision'

Actually, it is the leader of the Chaldean/Babylonians here who is doing all the scoffing, yes, it is Nebuchadnezzar who is jibing in mocking contempt at the opposing Kings and the Judean one in particular. Indeed, even the Jewish 'hotspurs' among the young men, the princes and captains, the muscle men full of patriotism and testosterone, like stallions, neighing for battle, are also simply sniffed at as being some piece of insignificant dung on the bottom of a Chaldean sandal. The Hotspurs are then in turn, also publicly sneered and jeered and laughed at. This raucous ribbing then finally goes on to ridicule Jerusalem's great ramparts of resistance, for the Chaldeans will simply take the dust of the ground, pile it up against them, and march on over it, for the Chaldeans, you see, shall take the land off their enemies and turn even their beloved soil against them.

Habakkuk 1:10

They scoff at kings, And princes are scorned by them. They deride every stronghold, For they heap up earthen mounds and seize it. Then his mind changes, and he transgresses; He commits offense, Ascribing this power to his god. NKJV

I am old enough to have seen this triple set of attorneys manifest themselves in many individuals. The beginning and ongoing successes have always eventually turned to disaster for such people. Why? Because sooner or later, such individuals become 'full of themselves'; they begin to believe their own press and they are fooled into thinking such permissive power has emanated essentially from themselves, and that such good fortune and bright favor has been generated by the engines of their own devices. In our present day, these three attorneys mostly represent the god of self. In the time of the Chaldeans, they represented the manifestation of many demon gods, and the Chaldeans worshipped them. Remember: what you sacrifice to, that you worship- even today.

See the progression here? God permits the Chaldeans power to possess that which is not theirs. They do it with furious aplomb. However, with each victory comes not only expanse of territory but expanse of pride, and pride my friends, deceives. Such prideful expansion, it seems, will always, and I mean always, force the expresser to overstep permissive boundaries and thereby cause to bring into their own houses, a ruinous offence, the greatest of these being to finally make God their enemy and the source of their own retributive judgment.

Now then dear reader, whenever you see these three attorneys,(Scoff, Scorn and Derision) be assured they are going to get their clients hung. Make sure that they are never on your case

When Scoff, Scorn and Derision are let loose in their fullness, they always 'big up' a person way beyond the valleys of self preservation and up into the high mountains of destruction. It is Habakkuk's observation of this ignorant and haughty movement into self actualization and self deception which shall now move the prophet in close to God with a deity-winkling question regarding His intent toward such arrogance.

Now then dear reader, whenever you see these three attorneys, be assured they are going to get their clients hung. Make sure that they are never on your case.

Listen: *Pride goes before destruction, And a haughty spirit before a fall. Proverbs 16:18 NKJV*

Pray: Lord, right now, we humble ourselves before You. Have mercy upon us O God for not acknowledging and thanking You for all Your manifold goodness toward us. When we become the instrument of Your providence, help us to acknowledge our usefulness and power to be from You. Amen and let it be so.

Bible Insight 16

Night-Whisper | DARE

Incredulous intercession and the corrosive Chaldeans

Habakkuk knows the sinfulness of his own people. As a seer, he has also been allowed to see the judgment which God is going to bring upon them. However, and further still, he has also been able to see the glittering and terrifying sword of that judgment begin to rust and rot before his face, revealing its dirty and jagged rusted edges. The Chaldeans are self-corrosive.

Habakkuk 1:12

re You not from everlasting, O Lord my God, my Holy One? We shall not die. O Lord, You have appointed them for judgment; O Rock, You have marked them for correction. NKJV

So, from this terrible and now confusing vision of a warped sword of judgment, Habakkuk turns again to face the ears of the Lord and intercede with some happy incredulity! Though this is a "You've got to be kidding me? Right?" kind of prayer, Habakkuk's deliverance of it, testifies that he has at last found a solid place to then stand and wait for God to answer. Habakkuk, you see, knows that after this prayer, frankly, there is nothing more to be said, for he is calling on the Pure and Holy Rock of Righteous Judgment to respond to His own eternal declaration and unalterable response to the Chaldean's idolatrous pride: "I will bring you down."

'Incredulity', you see, is the name above that archway of the unsought for entrance to the garden of God. So, be sure of this, when we perceive a seeming inconsistency in action, or reaction of God, then it is time to turn and look for that hidden archway and that open-mouthed doorway of 'incredulity'. When you see it, then go through it quickly, running, smiling and shaking your head, and though you find no green grass to sit or kneel on in this part of the garden of God, you shall nevertheless find many an ageless and immovable rock to set your quivering legs upon. Stand still on them and just wait there now there my friends, yes, stand on the unchanging statements of the character and intention of God and you shall find that it is these very rocks which you are stood upon which become the big buzzers of God's doorbell and that by and by, God Himself will come to answer. Habakkuk had found this incredulous inconsistency and was happy. The sword shall at least be broken across the backs of those it strikes in judgment.

There are times in our lives, when regarding the happenings in the life of a person, a situation, an event or a circumstance, that our spirit cries out, "No this cannot be! God is not like this!" When this happens, maybe a worm-hole of incredulity has opened up in the high - walled garden of God Most High. If so, go through it. Find some statements of the character and intent of God that are contrary to those happenings you are experiencing and then stand on them. Proclaim the Rock's solid and essential and unchanging nature, say: "You are the faithful God. O Lord, You are holy. Father You are good and gracious, slow to anger and abundant in steadfast loving kindness! Father you are light and not darkness! God you are good and not evil! You, O God have said, I will never leave you not forsake you, therefore…..," and so on, and so forth.

> *Where prayer and God are concerned, incredulity is in fact an unexpected and delightful gift, a worm-hold opening into the rock garden of the Lord.*

Stand there and watch. Be quiet now and wait. Listen up and look. God will come with an answer.

Where prayer and God are concerned, incredulity is in fact an unexpected and delightful gift, a worm-hold opening into the rock garden of the Lord.

Listen: *Then He spoke a parable to them, that men always ought to pray and not lose heart, Luke 18:1NKJV*

Pray: Father we look for solid ground to stand upon which to offer You our prayers. Your Son our Savior is our solid ground, the bright and blood red Rock upon which we stand. Your very name is our solid ground. Your character, Your declarations, Your intent, Your Fatherhood. Upon all of these we stand and pray today. Hear us O then, our Great God. Amen and let it be so.

Bible Insight 17

Vanishing pride

I have said it before and I shall say it again: I am old enough to remember turning off the old black and white TV set and seeing the picture collapse into a bright dot in the centre of the screen before seeming to diminish and vanish into the infinite distance of the grey-green cathode ray tube. Distance has a vanishing point to our ever-searching eyes.

Habakkuk 1:12

Are You not from everlasting, O Lord my God, my Holy One? We shall not die. O Lord, You have appointed them for judgment; O Rock, You have marked them for correction. NKJV

As we stand on our own particular point on the time line and stare either as far back into time as we can see or as far into the future as our dreams or nightmares might carry us, we could also say that we peer from 'vanishing point to vanishing point', or as the Hebrew might express it: from everlasting to everlasting.

God is from everlasting. Like a large compass He stretches from the vanishing point to vanishing point and at each point along the line. He is fully present there, all at once, at the same time. Indeed, He is even before the historical eastward appearing vanishing point and after the westward disappearing future one, yes, God encompasses all and is in all.

God is from the before beginning. He is from the East. He is the unchanging and ever certain light of the day and Jesus is His bright and morning star! What God has decreed, will come to pass. What God has covenanted shall not be broken. What God has declared will not be found to be a lie. Therefore, Habakkuk bases his incredulous intercession now on the tried and tested, proved and not found wanting, historical revelation of the very person of God Himself: Jehovah. Following this, Habakkuk also immediately testifies regarding the unyielding and holy nature of Jehovah and then wraps it all in the associative cry of his own dear heart. "Are You not from everlasting, O Lord MY God, MY Holy One?" As Matthew Henry intimates, Habakkuk might be saying: "We are an offending people and You are an offended God. Yet, we are still Your offended people and you are still our offended God." I like that.

The Christian then may offend his heavenly Father, but He is still His heavenly Father to offend! Yes, the son may shame His heavenly Father, but He is still His heavenly Father's son! Do you see this? So, at all points then, and in any situation and in any land, yes, the blood bought believer, no matter in what shade of darkness he might find himself in, can always say, "Are You not from everlasting, O Lord MY God, MY Holy One?"

Habakkuk sees the truth of the situation. God shall preserve a remnant. Israel shall not utterly be wiped from the face of the earth.

We can and more than that, Habakkuk now intercedes with three most certain and fantastic, full faith declarations. Here they are:

We shall not die.

O Lord, You have appointed them for judgment.

O Rock, You have marked them for correction.

Habakkuk sees the truth of the situation. God shall preserve a remnant. Israel shall not utterly be wiped from the face of the earth. Further than this, just as the Nazis found out, the proud judgment swords are also appointed themselves for judgment! Unlike Israel, they shall disappear forever! Indeed, in Germany of old, even the Swastika, that emblem of a once all-conquering regime, eventually became that very mark of international contempt, which caused both the former wearers and its acceptable use, to be removed from history forever. So shall God always deal in such a way with the proud people of this planet.

Listen: *The pride of your heart has deceived you, You who dwell in the clefts of the rock, Whose habitation is high; You who say in your heart, 'Who will bring me down to the ground?' Though you ascend as high as the eagle, And though you set your nest among the stars, From there I will bring you down," says the Lord. NKJV Obadiah 3-4*

Pray: Lord, before you have to humble me, I humble myself before You of King of ages and Lord of all. Father, thank You that You are faithful and despite my waywardness and willfulness, You are still my Father and I am still Your son. So then O Lord might we always say from any pig trough: "I will arise and go to my Father and say, Father…."

Bible Insight 18

The ineffably fearful mercy, in the corners of God's white eyes

Toward the end of Habakkuk Chapter 1, the prophet begins his enormous three question step climb towards his watchtower waiting place. He begins the climb with a statement: "You are of purer eyes than to behold evil, and cannot look on wickedness." Is this statement true?

Habakkuk 1:13-17

You are of purer eyes than to behold evil, And cannot look on wickedness. Why do You look on those who deal treacherously, And hold Your tongue when the wicked devours A person more righteous than he? Why do You make men like fish of the sea, Like creeping things that have no ruler over them? They take up all of them with a hook, They catch them in their net, And gather them in their dragnet. Therefore they rejoice and are glad. Therefore they sacrifice to their net, And burn incense to their dragnet; Because by them their share is sumptuous And their food plentiful. Shall they therefore empty their net, And continue to slay nations without pity? NKJV

I ask this because in my short sojourn of over half a century on this planet, through media communication and personal observation, I have beheld a torrent of ever flowing evil and wickedness from humanity at large, and frankly, let's not even go to the double springs of my own heart and the foul brackish water that has risen up in there over the years. In addition to this, since Adam and Eve took their bite at becoming gods, evil and wickedness have covered the earth like an overflowing turd filled toilet. Either then God has stopped looking or He has beheld the floating foulness 24 hours a day 7 days a week. If it is the latter, then surely He must be sick of it by now?

Imagine, if you will, a man turning his head away to the left in disgust and revulsion, whilst bringing the back of his left hand up to cover the right side of his mouth and nose, his eyes now moving to the right, still squinting at the sorry sight of his so great offence. In the same way, God does not look 'straight on' at sin, but rather, in sideways looking, the corner of His eyes now display the pure whites of inexpressible mercy toward the sinner, while at the same time His visage still expresses His most utter disgust at the sin. This is great mercy, for sin in the presence of God you see, usually brings only one ultimate double-barrel response: Judgment and punishment.

It seems to me then that God's mercy toward sinners means that the righteous will suffer. So, tell me now: how does this shape your prayer life?

While we then remember that the time of the full faced turning head of God toward our foul and floating turds gets nearer every day, let us be very thankful that God is presently more super abundantly gracious and merciful than He is disgusted and reviled. However, let us also remember that when His rising revulsion does turn His face toward the offending objects, then His wrath, like an all consuming irresistible molten lava, will be poured forth across the planet.

The prophet's first and second questions focuses never the less on God's all seeing sideway glancing. In other words, though God is not looking 'directly' at sin, He is still totally beholding sin and seemingly letting it go 'unanswered'. So in a strange twist in the theology of love, God's mercy toward sinners, even in judgment, seems to make space for the righteous to suffer as well! Yes, in His present mercy toward sinners then, Christians are dragged toward the judgment seat of the ungodly. In His present mercy toward sinners then, the hungry lions open their jaws upon the bowed heads of tear-trembling and urine soaked saints. In His mercy toward sinners then, the scimitar sword still beheads the dispossessed brethren. In His present mercy toward sinners then, the devil and his demonized henchmen devour the righteous in torture and burning; all the while, the disgusted Lord still mercifully holds His peace and keeps His sword sheathed most firmly at His side. "Why do You look on those who deal treacherously, and hold Your tongue when the wicked devours A person more righteous than he?" Why indeed.

It seems to me then that God's mercy toward sinners means that the righteous will suffer. So, tell me now: how does this shape your prayer life?

Listen: *He looks on the earth, and it trembles; He touches the hills, and they smoke. I will sing to the Lord as long as I live; I will sing praise to my God while I have my being. May my meditation be sweet to Him; I will be glad in the Lord. May sinners be consumed from the* *earth, And the wicked be no more. Bless the Lord, O my soul! Praise the Lord! Psalms 104:32-35 NKJV*

Pray: Lord, spare the righteous! When you look to present and general judgment, please spare the righteous. Don't let us be washed away with the wicked in the time of Noah, or murdered like Cain. Don't let us be brimstone bombed from our houses, or our legs landmine ripped from our bodies. Don't let us suffer with the wicked at the hands of the wicked. In all your forward looking, in Your wrath, remember mercy toward your children still living in the cities of Sodom and the ghastly places of Gomorrah. Amen and let it be so.

Bible Insight 19

The prophet's position

A long time ago, on the planes of Mamre, Abraham was quite literally shooting the breeze in the heat of the day. Whilst sat at his open tent flap door, three beings disguised as men were seen passing by. Abraham persuaded all three to engage in his hospitality and in the so doing, he entertained angels unawares. Now one of these beings was the pre-incarnate Lord Himself, and the other two, a pair of SAS angels on a snatch and destroy mission to Sodom. It is often said in the media today that Jesus said nothing about homosexuality. Well, in Genesis 18, He is on His way to destroy a couple of cities because of it and its seemingly perpetual smoking of the aftermath, would be seen for centuries to come in the dead sea area of the Jordan rift valley.

Habakkuk 2:1

I will stand my watch And set myself on the rampart, And watch to see what He will say to me, And what I will answer when I am corrected. NKJV

Now then, Abraham rushed to refresh the hearts of these three strangers and once he had hastily prepared their meal, he stood by them, like some silver-service waiter ready to attend to their every need.

"So he took butter and milk and the calf which he had prepared, and set it before them; and he stood by them under the tree as they ate." Genesis 18:8

Now I mention this verse in Genesis today for two reasons, first, regarding Abraham's acts of hospitality and service. Abraham had his suspicion who these beings were and where they were from. So, he was expectant in his waiting; indeed Abraham clearly expected a reward for his hospitality and service. Even an angels reward, even a prophet's reward, even a reward from the hand of the Lord! For this reward, whatever God deemed it to be he 'stood' by them for it and waited. In Abraham's case of course, that reward was the affirmation of God's promise of a son, the strengthening of Sarai to believe for it and in the end, the arrival of baby Isaac himself!

The second reason I mention this incident is the word used for 'stood' or 'standing' by them, in Genesis 18:8 it is the same word used here in Habakkuk. The prophet Habakkuk therefore 'stood' with great expectation before the Lord. His question had been asked, his praise and complaint had been given (so like us) and now he stood with great expectation.

As an old sailor in the Royal Navy, I am used to four-hour watches with a two-hour dogwatch covering varying cycles. Whatever the watch system utilized at sea however, the purpose is the same: To keep the boat functioning and fully operational twenty-four hours per day. So when Abraham's son Isaac later experienced a great famine in the land of his living, he was tempted to go back to Egypt. God came to Isaac and said "No! You shall not go. Stay where you are and I will protect and provide for you, bless you and make your descendents be multiplied and give you the land I promised to your father Abraham" and in the so saying, God also explained that He would do this "because Abraham obeyed My voice and kept My charge, My commandments, My statutes, and My laws" Genesis 26:5. That is, Abraham kept my 'watch' or 'charge' (same word).

The main mark of the man of God is essentially one of faithful expectancy. Are you standing your watch tonight?

So for tonight then friend be sure of these two great truths: You have your 'watch,' you have your set period of time to be alert and to be attentive, to be useful and to be faithful.

If you are alive, then you are still on your 'watch', the length of which is still unknown to you, for the watch change ending of your expectant life is in the hands of the Master of the boat. Now then, I say 'expectant' because you must stand your watch, that is, you must be looking to the Lord of your watch with expectancy. What have you asked for? Look for it! What have you dreamed for? Hope for it! What have you desired from the Lord? Long for it with the expectancy of soon to be satisfied sailor.

The main mark of the man of God is essentially one of faithful expectancy. Are you standing your watch tonight?

Listen: *Let a man so consider us, as servants of Christ and stewards of the mysteries of God. Moreover it is required in stewards that one be found faithful. 1 Corinthians 4:1-2NKJV*

Pray: I have kept Your word O Lord. I have served You with my whole heart. I have sacrificed my all to You my God and opened wide the door of my tent. I stand my watch O Lord. I wait for You to come. Speak Lord in the stillness, while I wait on thee, hushed my heart to listen, in expectancy. Amen.

Bible Insight 20

Night-Whisper | MASTERY

The prophet's penthouse

Habakkuk 2:1

*I will stand my watch
And set myself on the
rampart, And watch to
see what He will say to
me, And what I will
answer when I am
corrected. NKJV*

The seer of the Lord with expectant faithfulness positions himself in the place of receiving an answer. He will 'set himself on the rampart' that is, just like Miriam watched from the shore of the Nile to see what would happen to the baby Moses, so Habakkuk would watch to see the redemption of the remnant from the river of judgment. Yes, like the grown man Moses would later stand before Pharaoh and deliver the bondage breaking command of the Lord, so Habakkuk would stand before the King of Kings, even in the royal court of the prayers of his supplication and wait for an answer. Habakkuk then, in his heart, set himself in a particular position to receive from the Lord. He was on the shores of deliverance; He was in the Royal courts of the great King. Watchman of God! How about you then? Have you set your faithful and expectant feet in the same ground as Habakkuk? Have you withdrawn from all distraction to turn your eyes inward to the high temple place of the Spirit of the Lord within you? Have you ascended the inner heights? Have you risen above anxiety? Have you left the yapping dogs of temporal demands and the daily distractions beneath you? Are you above the general disdain for all things unseen? Have you come apart, come alone, come expectant to serve and wait on God? Are you yet above the clamor? Are you yet above the crowd? Are you yet above the hand clapping and the back patting yet? Are you above the mere men below and now alone and exposed only to God on high?

Whether rampart, wall or tower, Habakkuk was alone, watching and waiting on the Lord, looking for a runner to appear on the high inner hills of his looking, waiting for that messenger from heaven to appear on the horizon of his watching soul, and when seen, mark well now, when seen, to quickly welcome his arrival and receive the heavy breathed out message which would be so heaving and heart- pumpingly powerfully delivered into his being. For when the runner from heaven is seen, the message shall be delivered quickly, imminently, instantly, immediately. Yes, when a message is once seen in the distance, it is often then delivered speedily and with an heaving force upon the face of the watching heart. It is seen and heard, but mostly it is felt, yes, it is received in your bosom like a hit from a charging linebacker.

> *When the runner from heaven is seen, the message is seen and heard, but mostly it is felt, yes, it is received in your bosom like a hit from a charging linebacker*

Habakkuk had made his complaint and laid out his questions before the Lord. He cared not whether he would be rebuked. He minded not if he might be chastened. These were not the issues. He was in the loving hands of his heavenly Father and whether God's answer was soft or sharp, it was God's answer he was most earnestly looking for.

The prophet waits with faithful expectancy, willing to receive whatever God may say. Man of God; I say, man of God! Are you doing the same tonight?

Listen: *Unto You I lift up my eyes, O You who dwell in the heavens. Behold, as the eyes of servants look to the hand of their masters, As the eyes of a maid to the hand of her mistress, So our eyes look to the Lord our God, Until He has mercy on us. Have mercy on us, O Lord, have mercy on us! For we are exceedingly filled with contempt. Our soul is exceedingly filled With the scorn of those who are at ease, With the contempt of the proud. Psalms 123 NKJV*

Pray: I am faithful to my calling O God. I do not waiver, neither do I doubt. I have ascended my high hill O Lord. I am watching, I am waiting, I am ready. Speak Lord in the stillness, while I wait on thee, hushed my heart to listen, in expectancy. Amen.

Bible Insight 21

The watchtower of waiting

Remember then that the prophet Habakkuk is having what we might call, a 'crisis of faith.' In other words, he has seen what the proud, self-possessed and brutal army of the Chaldean's, God's sword of judgment, shall do to his people and he just cannot match this up with his understanding of the pure nature of God. Therefore, he has gone above the cry and clamor of the city and especially the whirlpool sucking of his own now very turbulent soul and mind, and is now waiting to see what God will say to Him. Yes, Habakkuk is making watchtower space to wait for the whisper of the still small voice of God within him. Then and now, God speaks to His people in five distinct ways:

Habakkuk 2:1

I will stand my watch And set myself on the rampart, And watch to see what He will say to me, And what I will answer when I am corrected. NKJV

1. By His Spirit through His Word.

2. By His Spirit through our conscience.

3. By His spirit through His providence.

4. By His spirit through His people.

5. By His spirit through God interpreted pictures.

The end of this speaking shall be for us all, at the very least, an almost physically felt movement in the very centre of our being, for the breathed out whisper of God is the most powerful force in the universe and in us, it is most surely felt. One Word spoken from Him, you see, changes everything in earth and heaven and in the countless unseen vast dimensions. Just one word. It's worth waiting for, and certainly for Habakkuk the word he receives shall salve his heart, solve the difficulties in his mind and strengthen him for the challenges to come.

I am sure that Habakkuk did not arrive on top of his own watchtower to then calmly sit in the 'lotus position.' He is obviously agitated, frustrated and confused. Even so, and this is very important, he has now wrestled himself into a waiting stillness and it has been an energetic struggle as well, for it has involved an emotional emptying; it has involved an eviction of the violent doubting of his mind, together with a binding and gagging of the words and works of his unbelieving flesh. The watchtower for Habakkuk may well have been an external and physical place, but essentially our watchtowers are always set on the internal mountain ranges of delectable watching. Yes, our watchtowers, you see, are within, and we often have to fight within ourselves to finally get on top of them.

The watchtower for Habakkuk may well have been an external and physical place, but essentially our watchtowers are always set on the internal mountain ranges of delectable watching.

Habakkuk arrives atop his tower for a single purpose: to see what God will say to him in answer to his complaint. This is the essential meaning of the last part of this verse for today.

Therefore be sure of this, that the exit road from 'Doubting Castle' will always lead to the delectable mountains, and for those that really want to see, 'Mount Clear' is the peak to peek into 'Emmanuel's Land'. Tell me then dear friend tonight, where are your watchtowers and have you ascended your own delectable internal mountain ranges to gain a view of the world to come? Even to quietly wait for the voice of the Lord?

Get your climbing boots on friend, for Mount Clear is worth the ascent!

Listen: *"By this time the pilgrims had a desire to go forwards, and the shepherds a desire they should; so they walked together towards the end of the mountains. Then said the shepherds one to another, "Let us here show to the pilgrims the gates of the Celestial City, if they have skill to look through our perspective glass." The pilgrims then lovingly accepted the motion: so they had them to the top of a high hill, called "Clear," and gave them their glass to look. Then they essayed to look; but the remembrance of that last thing that the shepherds had showed them made their hands shake, by means of which impediment, they could not look steadily through the glass: yet they thought they saw* *something like the gate, and also some of the glory of the place. Then they went away, and sang this song:*

'Thus by the shepherds secrets are revealed,

Which from all other men are kept concealed:

Come to the shepherds, then, if you would see

Things deep, things hid, and that mysterious be.' "

Pilgrims Progress – John Bunyan – Section 8

Pray: Lord, my heart is not haughty, Nor my eyes lofty. Neither do I concern myself with great matters, Nor with things too profound for me. Surely I have calmed and quieted my soul, Like a weaned child with his mother; Like a weaned child is my soul within me. O Israel, hope in the Lord, From this time forth and forever. Psalms 131 NKJV

Bible Insight 22

Night-Whisper | STRENGTH

Get up and get to it!

Then "the Lord answered me and said:" Now then, are not these words some of the most encouraging ones found in the Scriptures? The prophet asked. The prophet positioned himself. The prophet waited. The prophet heard. People today are purchasing flights to the other side of the world to get to some latest 'outpouring' or to some 'open heaven' insight, or some 'revival' to be able to hear from God! But if we would only ascend our own internal watchtower and wait on God we would hear a word from God for ourselves.

Habakkuk 2:2-30

And YHWH answered me, and said, "Write the vision, and make it plain upon tablets, that he may run that reads it. For the vision is yet for an appointed time, but at the end it shall speak, and not lie, though it hold back, wait for it; because it will surely come, it will not delay..." (NSB)

Dear friend, it is not that God is not speaking but rather, we His children are not taking the time to listen. Would a poor human parent fail to give advice to their own self-quieted, watching and waiting respectful little child? Of course not! Is God any less of a parent than we poor wretches? Of course not! The main problem I think is that watchtower climbing takes daily discipline and precious time.

Let us face facts that the demands of the day, of our jobs, of our children, of the media, of entertainment are unrelenting bullies. Indeed, it seems that there is not enough hours in the day nor enough energy in us to meet all of their searching and ever looking demands. Acknowledging that fact, Jesus Himself, never the less, left us a watchtower model for us to follow.

"Now in the morning, having risen a long while before daylight, He went out and departed to a solitary place; and there He prayed. And

Simon and those who were with Him searched for Him. When they found Him, they said to Him, "Everyone is looking for You."" Mark 1:35-37

There was no one as busy as Jesus. The spiritual and physical demands upon Him were gargantuan! How did He then, as the God-man, 'cope' and model for us all the way to proceed to our own watchtowers of waiting prayer? Well it simple really. He got up. He got out. He got to it.

Jesus literally MADE time to pray. Like a master carpenter, this great sculptor of time, carved out a daily niche of it in the wood of the coming day.

Years ago, I remember doing some outdoor assessment training on an upper Yardman's –pre-officer training course in the Brecon Beacons of South Wales. It was demanding and it was exhausting and I was glad to get back to my pup tent and sleeping bag. Late one night a small cadre of Royal Marine Commandoes slipped into our camp. They quietly pitched their tent, took care of their weapons and settled down for the night. I remember being woken up very early the next morning to get on with the days exertions and looked over to the place where the Commandoes were sleeping. They were gone and there was no trace that they had ever been there. A long time before the day they had arisen and quietly slipped away.

Listen now, Jesus literally MADE time to pray. Like a master carpenter, this great sculptor of time, carved out a daily niche of it in the wood of the coming day. Remember, that in the Bible, the day starts at 6:00am, so, when Jesus rises up a great while before daylight, be sure that it is still night. The stars are out. Now, take into account that the fourth watch of the night started at 3:00 am and it's not unreasonable to see the Lord was rising for prayer following this time.

Forget the accusations of legalism and all your whining excuses now. If you want to be great in God, if you want to hear from Him, then get up early, a long while before daylight and ascend your watchtower. Pay the price. Be elite. GET UP A GREAT WHILE BEFORE THE DAY AND GET ON WITH IT. People do this and they do not die. They just go to bed earlier. So then my friend, I say to you today: Live your life differently. Get up from your bed. Get up to your watchtower and listen and pray. Maybe then the Lord will answer you and say……

Listen: *Give ear to my words, O Lord, Consider my meditation. Give heed to the voice of my cry, My King and my God, For to You I will*

*pray. My voice You shall hear in the morning, O Lord; In the morning
I will direct it to You, And I will look up. Psalms 5:1-3NKJV*

Pray: Lord, I give you my mind and my body. Father, I give you my time
and my sleep. Now then Father God speak to me your servant and show
me great and mighty things that for now I do not now. Speak Lord for
Your servant is listening. Amen.

Bible Insight 23

Hardy Heralds

God now commands Habakkuk to write down what he sees. A vision written is a vision preserved, a vision shared, a vision seen by many eyes, a vision examined, a vision discerned. Write down the vision. For long time now we have had access to pen and the paper, and even lately to mobile word processors, so, there is no excuse that we cannot write down what we too have seen from God, have heard from God, have received on our own watchtowers of looking. Are you writing down what God has revealed to you? Are you keeping a 'prophetic' journal? Orders re-read are often orders revisited which shall then be most certainly be acted upon. Promises re-read produce solid ground underneath standing feet once found sinking. Warnings remembered will keep us on the straight and narrow. Tell me then, do you have a watchtower journal?

Habakkuk 2:2-3

And YHWH answered me, and said, "Write the vision, and make it plain upon tablets, that he may run that reads it. For the vision is yet for an appointed time, but at the end it shall speak, and not lie, though it hold back, wait for it; because it will surely come, it will not delay..." (NSB)

Habakkuk was told to make the writing 'plain and on tablets'. There are to be no ciphers here, no subtext, no 'in between the lines' exposés, just plain and understandable text. In today's terms we might say, 'Use plain language and a good sized, easy to read bold enabled font.' Dig out the lines of each letter. Make them deep and long lasting, for the vision you see now Habakkuk will take some time to come. Now then, remember that just because God gives you a vision today, it does not mean that it will be fulfilled tomorrow. Make your writing plain then. Least not, that you yourself do not forget or misinterpret the reading of them in the future. As a writer, far too often I have a read over old notes and repeated the lines "What on earth was I on about here?" Where the notes are not understood, the message becomes meaningless and the initial vision is lost forever. So dear 'journaler' and victorious vision writer: be sure to dig out your plain letters to make visible and understandable for the appointed time. So, Habakkuk did not have to make the writing plain for people to read when they were literally running from the Chaldeans. No, that would be a little ridiculous and very late coming. Habakkuk meant that discernment of the same vision now written down would come as people's eyes ran over it, yes, as they studiously and prayerfully, most carefully considered the text. The Word of God is not to be read whilst on the run from coffee shop to train station, from the office to 'going home' car, from early morning bedroom to 9:00am boardroom. No, such trifling over the text will only leave you wobbly in your faith through the osteoporosis of the inner man, and to such an extent, that you will become an 'evanjellyfish'! A boneless, structure-less individual, abandoned on the hot beach only to be pecked at by gannets! Just a nutrition-less piece of baby food, picked at by a baby's fork. Let your eyes run, and run again over the plain and preserved words of Scripture for therein is the calcium needed by your inner man. If you want to stand firm, then you must run your eyes over the Word of God, again and again and again.

The purpose of a strong spiritual bone structure is that you might also run.

The purpose of a strong spiritual bone structure is that you might also run. Once you understand the message, run to explain it and share it with others. Solid words, rightly received and understood, produce hardy heralds of the same. Never forget that the Bible is a plain message, a permanent message and a public message. Now, go run with it!

Listen: *Be diligent to present yourself approved to God, a worker who does not need to be ashamed, rightly dividing the word of truth. 2 Timothy 2:1NKJV*

Pray: Lord help me to have a loving desire, a constant hunger for You and Your most holy word. Amen and let it be so.

Bible Insight 24

In God's good time

I believe it has rightly been said that the prophetic word might not only has a personal and somewhat shadowy 'devotional' application for the readers present circumstance, but also has a literal and near application or near fulfillment to the time of proclamation, as well as a future application and fulfillment. So then, re-reading our text for today, our hearts might be 'devotionally warmed' about some personal matter which God has spoken to us about in our own 'long ago,' which He is now about to bring to pass in our own 'very soon.' Do you see this? In light of this, and let me be very careful here, you don't necessarily need to read the Bible to have such a 'devotional and spiritual affirmation.' Do you? For God could quite easily intimate this devotional affirmation to our inner man via a multitude of direct or indirect means. Never the less, God does seem often to use the Word of God in what I might call

Habakkuk 2:2-3

And YHWH answered me, and said, "Write the vision, and make it plain upon tablets, that he may run that reads it. For the vision is yet for an appointed time, but at the end it shall speak, and not lie, though it hold back, wait for it; because it will surely come, it will not delay..." (NSB)

this 'devotional' manner. Such devotional fancies, as some might call them, may very well be rooted in solid facts however, and such devotional fancies may also be just that, you know, fancies! It is only a maturity in God and a thorough acquaintance with the Word of God which, will protect you from the sickly sweet selfishness so often found in such fancies which are not based on the facts of God's revealed character and true promises but simply upon our devotional understanding of them. Do not discount the warming of the heart and affirmation of the Holy Spirit within you, but do be careful how you read.

Now this particular vision we know, had an immediate application to both the Chaldean/Babylonian captivity and its ultimate end. However, the writer to the Hebrews directed by the Holy Spirit, personifies the vision in the very person of Christ, saying to the then Hebrew reader and to us maybe considering drawing back Christians in need of succor and staying power: "For you have need of endurance, so that after you have done the will of God, you may receive the promise: 'For yet a little while, And He who is coming will come and will not tarry. Now the just shall live by faith; But if anyone draws back, My soul has no pleasure in him.' But we are not of those who draw back to perdition, but of those who believe to the saving of the soul." Hebrews 10:36-39 NKJV

God's clock is immovable and unstoppable, it is un-hasting and unrelenting, ever ticking past and activating a multitude of different alarm settings. God's timing however, is not our timing.

So Habakkuk's written vision, whilst having a near application and fulfillment is also prophetically transposed from the Babylonian captivity and the application of faithful patience, hundreds of years hence to the drawing back Hebrew Diaspora and then thousands of years into the future to us; to me; to you! This vision then rings out to all of Christ's battling and sometimes beleaguered church: "Jesus is coming back for us! Don't give up hope. Don't cease from doing good and pleasing the Father. Have faith. All will be well. It's going to be worth it! For just as salvation from the Babylonians came, and with it a coming again to Jerusalem, so shall your deliverance from present trouble come and Jesus will also come and take you to the city of God, the mother of us all, the New Jerusalem of free men and women in heaven above! All will happen, just as God has said and in His most perfect time. In the meanwhile then, live by faith in God's most certain word. "

God's clock is immovable and unstoppable, it is un-hasting and unrelenting, ever ticking past and activating a multitude of different alarm settings. God's timing however, is not our timing. Even so, in God's good time, never early nor never late, what He has said and purposed shall surely come to pass, yes, it will surely come.

Habakkuk's vision was to declare their guilt, highlight their danger and point to their deliverance through faith in the gracious actions of their God! With faith and hope then, with love and joyful expectation, the saints have always both watched and waited for such certain salvation and hoped in the ever running words of this so great a declaration

Listen: *All scripture is given by inspiration of God, and is profitable for doctrine, for reproof, for correction, for instruction in righteousness:*

That the man of God may be perfect, throughly furnished unto all good works. 2 Timothy 3:16-17 KJV

Pray: Father, may the fact and the power of the truth of Your word become for me the fuel of all my living. Amen and let it be so.

Bible Insight 25

Night-Whisper | TRUTH

The Swollen soul of the bent and stone swallowing snake

Pride is the sin of sins, the root of all nasty lunacy, the bed of all falseness, the bending of all morals, the dark corrupting of all that is light. Pride is hard like a stone swallowed whole. It is heavy and unyielding in its warped self assessment and blinding in its bending of light. Plato rightly said something akin to: "straightness can only be truly measured when laid by the side of that which is knowingly or definingly straight and then touches it at every point." So, introduce a swallowed swelling into the body of that which is supposed to be straight and then lay it alongside the true measure of straightness and it will only touch the truth at the point of its hard and swollen fatness and the name of that point is 'judgment'. The thing is not straight. It is fat, swollen, warped, crooked, and bent, coiling in on its own power, judgment and wrong conclusions. It is snake like. It is not upright.

Habakkuk 2:4

Behold, his soul which is lifted up is not upright in him: but the just shall live by his faith. NKJV

Our souls are lifted up, when we do not believe God's Word. Our souls are lifted up when we mock God's prophets. Our souls are lifted up when such disbelief causes us not only to deny Divine words, but to act contrary to God's revelation and in the so doing, to put ourselves in danger of death and destruction. Do you see that? Pride leads to death and destruction.

Very few heeded the word of the Lord through Habakkuk's contemprary, the prophet Jeremiah. Therefore, they either died terribly, or were carried away into cruel bondage. This is what shall happen to the proud of heart.

Now then comes the clear contrast. The upright soul is just. It just believes God's word, even if, in the low valleys of their present looking, that word from heaven seems so contrary to what they presently see and experience. The just, just believe His word. In this immediate context, 'the just' who believe the word of the Lord through Jeremiah (Habakkuk's prophetic contemprary), shall escape the nastiness of Nebuchadnezzar and shall be delivered from the wrath to come and shall live! Adam Clarke summarily comments: "He that believes the promises of God and has found life through believing, shall live by his faith." So then, this statement becomes a universal statement, applicable to Jews and gentiles, that is, to the whole of mankind. "The just shall live by faith."

Christian, you must believe God's Holy word. You must live a straight and upright life as a testimony to your believing. If you do not do this, then you are still a self-deceived, bent blind fathead.

Those who believe the Gospel of the Lord Jesus Christ are counted then by God's grace as faithful and just, as forgiven and free, as alive and not dead. Those who do not believe the Gospel, continue to be in a bent and blind, hard, cold and fat crooked darkness. They are dead in their trespasses and sins, their appointment with the wrath to come, an un-hastening certainty'

Christian, you must believe God's Holy word. You must live a straight and upright life as a testimony to your believing. If you do not do this, then you are still a self-deceived, bent blind fathead.

Listen: *So they rose early in the morning and went out into the Wilderness of Tekoa; and as they went out, Jehoshaphat stood and said, "Hear me, O Judah and you inhabitants of Jerusalem: Believe in the Lord your God, and you shall be established; believe His prophets, and you shall prosper." 2 Chronicles 20:20 NKJV*

Pray: We sing to you our God, in praise we declare the resplendent beauty of your magnificent holiness. Praise You O our Father, for Your mercy endures forever. Ambush those who would harm us, break the crooked where they stand, come and wipe them from Your land and give the spoil to us, yes, take all the vast and stolen treasures of the darkness and freely give it to Your sons. So shall we bless You O Lord our God and return to Jerusalem and the house of our Lord with singing, for the rest and the peace we shall experience, shall have been bought and given to us by You, yes You alone, who have fought against our enemies and left them dead before us. Amen and let it be so.

Bible Insight 26

Night-Whisper | MASTERY

Dope on a rope

Now we turn to Nebuchadnezzar, the insatiably proud potentate of the Babylonian Kingdom, who is in himself a picture of the devil and also an example of all the machinations of proud intentions, institutions men and nations. What this verse says regarding him is very plain indeed.

Habakkuk 2:5

"Indeed, because he transgresses by wine, He is a proud man, And he does not stay at home. Because he enlarges his desire as hell, And he is like death, and cannot be satisfied, He gathers to himself all nations And heaps up for himself all peoples. NKJV

Pride, which mounts itself up on the backs of others, never ever satisfies the high seeking heart. When it is asked "How much is enough?" it always replies, "just a little more". Thus the Babylonian Kingdom headed by Nebuchadnezzar swallowed up the nations in hell consuming, wide-mouthed insatiability. In our nations right now, pride is exalting itself once more and thus also consuming itself in a similar wide-mouth hedonistic gluttony of every filthy thing.

Now it says of Nebuchadnezzar, that picture of pride incarnate, that "because he transgresses by wine, He is a proud man…" The picture here is one of mad, out of control drunkenness. Now, the old saying goes that 'God in His great goodness gave the grape to cheer both great and small. Little fools drink too much and great fools none at all,' and as the Bible is clear that wine if given to gladden the heart of man it is also clear about its most dangerous excesses. We must be aware, that there are only a few fluid ounces that are between the gladness of a little and the mocking of too much wine. If you wade into drunkenness and sin by a few fluid ounces, then you are not wise. 'Snake Bite,' you see, is much more than a brand name for some Southern Scrumpy my friend; that extra glass will bite you.

I have never forgotten being on 'Cell-watch duty' when being based in HMS Dolphin for my submarine training. In the late 1970's the biggest cause of death in the Royal Navy was drowning on your own drunken vomit. Thus, anyone arrested for drunkenness was put in cells both for the offense and also for their own safety. The young man who I watched one particular night, left his morning cell as quiet as a lamb, and yet was brought in the night before insane with drink and strapped to a stretcher. I remember the Naval Police quickly leaving the cell as they unstrapped him and the force of the freed man's anger as he threw the

All your excuses for any continuing drug use are simply that. Excuses!

stretcher against the bars and then prowled like a wolf, spitting vengeance, hatred, anger and all other manner of evil declarations out of his cesspit spewing mouth. I am glad he never followed through with those things he said he was going to do with me when he got out! Drunkenness, you see, is a gateway for darkness, a vehicle for all manner of evil to ride in and ride upon. Drunkenness you see, possesses you, it straps lying goggles of greatness across your own self vision and fills you with pride. Whether you are under the influence of weed, cocaine; heroine or wine, you are quite simply a sinning proud dope-head, ever seeking to possess that which is not yours, always dissatisfied with your lot, whose end shall be beastliness and brokenness, emptiness and loneliness.

If you have been saved from this in your past, why might you be returning as a dog to its vomit to temporary pleasures which have previously destroyed you? All your excuses for any continuing drug use are simply that. Excuses! If this is you, then humble yourself right now you proud self consuming dope-headed and silly little sinner. Come to Christ again right now, and He will set you free from all of your proud addictions. 'Fess up,' whilst there is still time. The Christian must be in control of himself and does that by being controlled by the Holy Spirit. Anything else is sin. Anything else is stupid. Anything else is pride and a falling death. Mark my words, if you are controlled by booze or drugs, on some kind of gallows somewhere, you will eventually swing for it.

Listen: *Who has woe? Who has sorrow? Who has contentions? Who has complaints? Who has wounds without cause? Who has redness of eyes? Those who linger long at the wine, Those who go in search of mixed wine. Do not look on the wine when it is red, When it sparkles in the cup, When it swirls around smoothly; At the last it bites like a serpent, And stings like a viper. Your eyes will see strange things, And your heart will utter perverse things. Yes, you will be like one who lies down in the midst of the sea, Or like one who lies at the top of the mast,*

saying: "They have struck me, but I was not hurt; They have beaten me, but I did not feel it. When shall I awake, that I may seek another
Proverbs 23:29-35 NKJV

Pray: Lord Jesus, come be our satisfaction. Amen and let it be so.

Bible Insight 27

Five woes sung by the choir of the dispossessed

The earth is the Lord's and the fullness thereof. Therefore for God to call Abraham and build up from him a people to possess so very small a portion of this earth, is completely according to His sovereign will and at His sovereign bequest. The land of Israel is that land apportioned to Israel.

Habakkuk 2:6-8

"Will not all these take up a proverb against him, And a taunting riddle against him, and say, 'Woe to him who increases What is not his — how long? And to him who loads himself with many pledges'? Will not your creditors rise up suddenly? Will they not awaken who oppress you? And you will become their booty. Because you have plundered many nations, All the remnant of the people shall plunder you, Because of men's blood And the violence of the land and the city, And of all who dwell in it. NKJV

The earth is the Lord's and fullness thereof. So, after the flood, the triple and general migration of the three sons of Noah began to apportion the boundaries of the coming nations. The judgment at Babel then further subdivided and separated people by tongue and ultimately even further by location, climate, culture and race. Humanity is one blood but consists of many nations of heavenly apportioned, geopolitical boundaries, and it is God who made it so. Apart from the land of Israel however, no one has come across a realtor's description of the boundaries of occupation and delineation for each and every nation of the earth. Add to this, the presence of sin in that particular form of national envy, and national greed and national revenge, together with the overlaid spiritual authorities and boundaries of the kingdom of darkness across the globe and what you have is a whole lot of trouble.

The United Nations, born out of one need to quell conquest and greed, plunder and poverty, or out of the plan to unite the nations under 'the man of sin' and against the plans of the Lord, is in any event, an oxymoron. Sin will never allow the unity of the nations in peace. The man of sin will never unite the nations in unity and peace. The Prince of Peace Himself is the only person that has the right and the power to do so; and He will.

Meanwhile the nations, in rapacious covetousness, heave and roar against one another and even though here in Habakkuk, the Chaldeans and the Babylonians are the sword of judgment against the people of God, they are responsible for their own actions and so subject to the full backwash of a sowing and reaping judgment against themselves.

God separates. Light and darkness, day and night, male and female, tribes and tongues and even nations, and as there is a place for the sun and the moon in the boundaries of the planetary heavens, so there is a place for male and female, for tongues and for tribes, yes, there is a place for national boundaries. Look now, even though all are one blood that together need to come under the redeeming blood of Jesus, in the so doing, male and female still remain, as do tribe and tongue, and all the God apportioned national geopolitical places on the surface of the planet. Unlike the 'Great Realtor's' defining boundaries for the nation of Israel, in all other nations, it is culture, climate and tongue that seem to be the triple indicators of those other 'natural' boundaries.

Still, despite these self-defining natural boundaries, nation still rises up against nation, and here, Babylon in particular is the great thief of the earth. She violently takes what is not hers to take. She spreads her desire and her legs, her nets and her tent pegs over peoples and places which are not hers.

Still, despite these self-defining natural boundaries, nation still rises up against nation, and here, Babylon in particular is the great thief of the earth. She violently takes what is not hers to take. She spreads her desire and her legs, her nets and her tent pegs over peoples and places which are not hers. She covets prominence and power, situation and treasure, resource and ungodly reward, for the purpose of the peaceful hedonistic consumerism of her own self-declared elite, and in the end, exist for the purpose of bringing forth 'the man of sin'.

All of this dear friends, is simply food for thought, for I personally cannot begin to unravel the complications of economic migration, the fleeing of persecution, immigration, subjugation, and the other problems of sinful mankind all mixed up with the interweaved machinations of the kingdom of darkness against the coming King of heaven. However, some facts are still facts and the five coming 'woes' here in Habakkuk, outline some very pertinent warnings for the nations of the earth and all else who set themselves against the Most High.

However, pray more, I say pray much, much more, that Christ, the Prince of Peace would come and through righteous war, establish a lasting and righteous peace, even a throne for His very pruning hook presence among us.

So then, you nations that have become proud and increasingly Godless, BEWARE! For though you have been the sword of God's judgment against other evils in the past, now God in turn will also judge you for your own sins against heaven and against humanity. Whoever you are then dear Christian, pray for that nation you find yourself humanly birthed in, that it might be a God fearing entity, acting righteously and compassionately, wisely and with great honor towards other nations of the earth. However, pray more, I say pray much, much more, that Christ, the Prince of Peace would come and through righteous war, establish a lasting and righteous peace, even a throne for His very pruning hook presence among us.

Listen: *He shall judge between the nations, and rebuke many people; They shall beat their swords into plowshares, And their spears into pruning hooks;Nation shall not lift up sword against nation, neither shall they learn war anymore. Isaiah 2:4*

Pray: Even so come Lord Jesus. Amen and let it be so.

Bible Insight 28

Woe one of five – The heavy clay of national rape

Adam Clarke, wonderfully imagines the captured nations of Nebuchadnezzar, now gathered together like one vast condemning choir, their lungs pumped up with such a vengeance that the five chorus of cursings which shall be chanted from their panting and poverty stricken person, shall pound the earth like broken arrows, even a full five times to his utter destruction.

Habakkuk 2:6-8

"Will not all these take up a proverb against him, And a taunting riddle against him, and say, 'Woe to him who increases What is not his — how long? And to him who loads himself with many pledges'? Will not your creditors rise up suddenly? Will they not awaken who oppress you? And you will become their booty. Because you have plundered many nations, All the remnant of the people shall plunder you, Because of men's blood And the violence of the land and the city, And of all who dwell in it. NKJV

For a nation to take what is not theirs to take is conquest and is plunder.

Now imagine such a thieving nation pictured like a man, every part of him so covered with riches that he cannot move. Each hand carries five bags of tightly packed gold coins, the handles of which are cutting off the blood supply at his wrists and biting big round red rings into the tops of his white and withering hands. Each of his shoulders are almost dissected with tied on treasure, and the big backpack of booty which he carries, bulges at the seams, the two-fold direction of the combined gravitational force being of such heaviness and of such a strain, that you don't know if it will either buckle his shaking knees or at any second, quickly flip him over on his back! So, as a counterbalance, his teeth are trying to bite into the handles of even more bags of silver and uncut diamonds, but they are so heavy that his jaw is stretched open wide, while at the same time, his fat belly bag and his many pocketed jacket all overflow with further plunder as his head also balances so many boxes of weighty delight, that he cannot take one more step. This man is increased beyond carrying capacity, he is laden with an immovable burden, he is clothed with heavy clay. Yes, like a payday loan company, he is insatiably hungry; yes, he is totally and utterly extortionate in his legalized robbery, his gross abuse and his malicious misuse of the unhappy situations of the destitute. Like a fat 'Cash Express' pawnbroker, he is ripping off the hungry, he is profiteering on despondency, and when they cannot pay, the bouncers are brought into play, and the bailiffs break through the doors, and the knuckle dustered wise guys spill the blood of the those that can no longer pay the protection racket of the potentates of stolen power.

And should the Prince of Peace tarry yet a little more, that nation now so proud, shall also disappear before the rising waves of a swelling and avenging humanity and be lost forever beneath the all-covering waves of history past.

Now, the poor sing out. The peoples have had enough. The plundered are done with their pledges. And as the power of the thief now wanes and he overstretches himself in maintaining his might, yes, as the pride of his fatness lulls him into slumber, the mad Medes cometh and powerful Persians are ready to reap the sowing of Nebuchadnezzar's sinful covetousness.

That nation, no matter how powerful, that nation who forgets God and refuses to humble themselves before Him, that nation who thinks their own might and power has delivered others into its hungry hands, that nation who has even been used as the sword of the Lord against another, that nation shall never the less fall! And should the Prince of Peace tarry yet a little more, that nation now so proud, shall also disappear before the rising waves of a swelling and avenging humanity and be lost forever beneath the all-covering waves of history past.

Listen: *"As a partridge that broods but does not hatch, So is he who gets riches, but not by right; It will leave him in the midst of his days, And at his end he will be a fool." Jeremiah 17:11 NKJV*

Pray: King of nations, Lord of all flesh, we bow ourselves before you. For all Your benefits we give you thanks. For all Your bounty we stand in awe. Let reparations be what they are and let them be fair and appropriate. However O Lord, help us to return that which was not ever ours to take. Help us to make restitution of that which was stolen and used. Help us to withdraw from places not assigned to us. Help us not to be power brokers, policemen of a world that is not ours, but like all good peoples, help us to stay at home and be happy in our lot, thankful in our own estate, always looking to You for protection and provision, for blessings and not cursing. amen and let it be so.

Bible Insight 29

Night-Whisper | DANGER

Woe one of five -Bite back time

The local Church of Scotland was given a gift by the neighboring mostly Pakistani filled Mosque to help buy new chairs for its failing congregation. Some months later that same Mosque approached the elders of the Kirk to get access to the church hall and the shiny new chairs, to present a series of public lectures on the heart and peaceful nature of Islam. They were not refused. People came, why wouldn't they, it was in the Kirk hall! All must be well.

Habakkuk 2:7,8

Shall they not rise up suddenly that shall bite thee, and awake that shall vex thee, and thou shalt be for booties unto them? Because thou hast spoiled many nations, all the remnant of the people shall spoil thee; because of men's blood, and for the violence of the land, of the city, and of all that dwell therein. KJV

Now whilst the word 'bite' here in the KJV has direct reference to the skin fanged and poisonous intrusion of a killer snake, its equal reference is to the interest rates placed on money loans. Those of us who had mortgages after the Black Monday stock market crash of the 1980's and those who even now live amongst economic and rising interest rates, know very well the financial stinging of the serpent that bites into your bank account at the end of each and every blood draining month. In greater measure of course, when it comes to servicing any national debt (that is paying back interest and any amount of initial and borrowed capital) then any interest rate rises on that national debt will mean that the money is harder to find and a default might well occur. When this happens at Sovereign nation level, financial bailiffs may seize that nations assets abroad or worst case, declare war. Yes, the nation that does not receive its payments may walk in and seize what it is owed, and then some. Nowadays of course, such interest rate led incursions are not obvious as they once were, and long before that a restructuring of the debt, indeed many restructurings of the debt may occur, much like a Mosque buying chairs for an old Kirk hall.

The restructuring of debt, of national financial favors come, nowadays, at quite a different national price. Look around you now. What nation now owns the buildings down your street? What nations now help influence and regulate your financial centers? What nations now have access to your schools and institutions? Which nations now have access to your research and to your nations' once so secret treasures? Mammon is no cheeky monkey, but it is a biting serpent, it is a squeezing python, whose dislocated jaw can swallow a nation whole. Those nations which have risen so seemingly suddenly around us, have risen up and bitten us on our booties. Past violence has given rise to this state of retribution. I wonder if national desperation may at some time try and re-write some global balance sheets.

Worse still, when ministries starve for lack of funds, and the people of God invest in the minor kingdoms of this world for their own future preservation sake, then the Kingdom of God has NOT come. Shame on us. Shame and laughable shame, that God's Kingdom is halted in its expanse because those Christians rich in this worlds goods, invest in rust and rot

Usury should not be found among the people of God. It is bondage. Shame on us when this happens. God's Kingdom has NOT come when such financial frame working is found among the people of God. Worse still, when ministries starve for lack of funds, and the people of God invest in the minor kingdoms of this world for their own future preservation sake, then the Kingdom of God has NOT come. Shame on us. Shame and laughable shame, that God's Kingdom is halted in its expanse because those Christians rich in this worlds goods, invest in rust and rot. I tell you, in this case my emaciated friends, we deserve all that we have got.

Listen: *Dan shall be a serpent by the way, A viper by the path, That bites the horse's heels So that its rider shall fall backward. I have waited for your salvation, O Lord! Genesis 49:17-18 NKJV*

Pray: Forgive your church O Lord for allowing itself to become a den of vipers. Have mercy upon us O God and help us to help ourselves, for even now, we have waited for Your salvation of Lord! Amen and let it be so.

Bible Insight 30

Night-Whisper | DEATH

Woe two of five - Of closed hearted fools

There is a train coming. It is the 5:40am dark mountain train from Mauthuasen to Ebensee. It runs like clockwork and it is never late.

Habakkuk 2:9-11

"Woe to him who covets evil gain for his house, That he may set his nest on high, That he may be delivered from the power of disaster! You give shameful counsel to your house, Cutting off many peoples, And sin against your soul. For the stone will cry out from the wall, And the beam from the timbers will answer it. NKJV

Mr & Mrs Herzgeschlossen love the mountains and their whole family are very rich. High up in the crystal clear air in just one day they have built their fine Super-Schloss. It is sumptuous, self-sufficient and exceptionally secure. Indeed, its position in the high mountains makes it unassailable. The valleys may suffer depravation and want, conquest and robbery, ahh, but here in the high mountains nested amidst the eagles, the Herzgesschlossen's Schloss is safe, is sure and is secure. The trouble is it is built directly upon the track which runs from Mauthuasen to Ebensee and its now 5:35am, and a screaming whistle is heard approaching from just around the bend, and remember now my friends, that the 5:40am dark mountain train is never late.

Every human contrivance, every human system is built essentially for protection, preservation and personal prosperity. From economic systems to arms and armies; from life insurance policies to burglar alarms; from bank savings for the rainy day; to roofs and walls; from safes and strong rooms to vitamin pills and raincoats. Whether it is against the elements, or against bad government, whether it is against the invasion of old age or of old enemies, all we build and invest in is essentially for protection and preservation. Like Mr and Mrs Blindheartedfool however, we all build our castles on the dark mountain track of the train of death and my friends, this train is never late, no, it is never deferred, no, it is never derailed and year on year the Doppler of its oncoming scream presses ever louder on our hand covered, headshaking, disbelieving little ear drums.

In this simple way, all we who make that nest, even though it be ever so fine, even though it be way up in the high hills of preventative protection, well, even there, we will always find that the dark mountain track runs straight through its centre, and the 5:40 Mauthuasen to Ebensee train is never late. One way or another, you see, in the first Adam, all die.

Meanwhile, of course, there is a train coming. It is the 5:40am dark mountain train from Mauthuasen to Ebensee. It runs like clockwork and it is never late

Outside of Christ, there is no hope of a future, no hope of a preservation or certainty of eternal life. In Christ, however, the last Adam, all live! Consequently then, there is no need to waste our lives building in the high hills of preventative protection. Even so, does the denominational stock market trading reflect this truth? Does independent, free church nepotism unknowingly frame this truth in a pack of family business preservation lies? Does the Bishop's Palace display this security? Do all our fat trusts extol such safety in Christ, and do all our bursting savings account sing to the world out this wonder of His daily provision toward us His children? Let's be honest here: Do we all truly believe this?

We need to ask ourselves and the Lord, where our wise ant-like provision and our scarlet clothed winter protection begin to erode the faith that we need to have in him. When does a good thing become a giant handicap to the obedience of faith? Surely it is good to have a store but surely it is better to know that our God is Jehova Jireh? Surely it is good to have a well provisioned army, but it is better to have God as our protector?

When the times come that out stores are empty and our boundaries are broken down, let us trust in the ever present goodness of the Lord and the immediate power of His might. I wonder, if that whenever our places of protection and provision become the replacements for our God, that the waters will rush in, overflow our banks, and ruin what we have put our trust in.

Meanwhile, of course, there is a train coming. It is the 5:40am dark mountain train from Mauthuasen to Ebensee. It runs like clockwork and it is never late.

Listen: *For as in Adam all die, even so in Christ all shall be made alive. 1 Corinthians 15:22*

Pray: So then O Lord, help us then to number our days and so live for You. Be then our protector and be them our protector both in our youth and in our age to come. Amen and let it be so.

Bible Insight 31

Night-Whisper | CONSIDER

Woe two of five – Shrieking stones and shivering timbers

It is going to be Nebuchadnezzar who seeks to make great his own house, that is, his own family and he shall do that at the great expense of others. So is the story of my own islands. So is the story of mankind in general.

Habakkuk 2:9-11

"Woe to him who covets evil gain for his house, That he may set his nest on high, That he may be delivered from the power of disaster! You give shameful counsel to your house, Cutting off many peoples, And sin against your soul. For the stone will cry out from the wall, And the beam from the timbers will answer it. NKJV

I am a free market man myself, but even so, when my financial freedom and family kingdom building means another person's slavery, then this causes much suffering and much cursing and such cursing is strong and re-percussive, and as usual, it seems to be written in two kinds of walls.

First, the walls of the victims. Though all created things may not have words, you see, they each still have a voice which speaks. Inanimate objects have very animate voices! God listens and will answer each and every one of these voices. Each cry from shed drops of blood, each shriek from a burnt ruin; each recorded horror from shocked and broken stone, even each testimony of terror squeezed from the gnarled knots of terrified timber, God hears and takes note of.

Secondly, the walls of the wealthy. The lush, plush edifices of Babylon were predominantly built on the conquest of covetousness and subsequent thievery. Not all, but most great houses in this world usually are! Being a true free market republican myself, I am always shocked at the wonder and awe painted on the faces of the comparative poor, as their rulers pass before them 'blinged' up to their eyeballs. Why do we take pride in the houses which rule us, which are built on nothing but ancient plunder and modern market manipulation? Be aware of this dear friend, ancient thievery still has present voices and God is still listening to them. Why are you really coveting after the same display? Why are you so enamored with celebrity of any kind? Could it be an outworking of personal covetousness? I think so.

Personally, I think the voices of inanimate objects, those condemning testimonies presented to us here as being from stones and beams, might be much more than a poetic and a literary device. Solid state organic memory is presently coming to the attention and advancement of current information storage and retrieval, and fanciful though it may well be, I wonder if we have still to plumb the depths of what is already recorded and stored in the intricate patterns of plants and planks, and of still waters and standing stones? The spiritual realm is not normally quiet, but fantastically noisy and full of voices speaking.

,Tell me Pastor. When did God's church become your very own family business and family inheritance? Tell me congregation, why are you allowing this?

So, there is nothing hidden and nothing unrecorded. All associated evidence shall be present at our soon and coming judgment. In light of this, dear Christian friends, let us make sure we all seek first God's Kingdom and His righteousness, for our treasure and our building shall all be tried by speaking fire, which in turn shall answer to its tasting: "wood, hay and stubble," or "gold silver and precious stones."

Finally, tell me Pastor. When did God's church become your very own family business and family inheritance? Tell me congregation, why are you allowing this?

Listen: *Then, as He was now drawing near the descent of the Mount of Olives, the whole multitude of the disciples began to rejoice and praise God with a loud voice for all the mighty works they had seen, saying: "'Blessed is the King who comes in the name of the Lord!' Peace in heaven and glory in the highest!" And some of the Pharisees called to Him from the crowd, "Teacher, rebuke Your disciples." But He answered and said to them, "I tell you that if these should keep silent, the stones would immediately cry out." Luke 19:37-40 NKJV*

Pray: Father, whilst in the side streets of vast unnumbered galaxies, homeless planets stand and sing Your praises around the midnight fires of spinning suns, and all creation still groans out the pains of its longing desires, whilst patiently waiting for the unveiling of the redeemed sons of the living God, we, the profoundly deaf, apologize for our corresponding personal muteness, and ask that You help us to both praise You now, for You are worthy of all our praise, and also help us leave a testimony of righteousness, that all Your creatures and Your creation would be blessed by it, and speak of it in the sunshine ages yet to come. Amen and let it be so.

Bible Insight 32

Woe three of five – The problem with blood, sweat and tears

Outside of when a nation is being used as the sword of the Lord in the direct judgment of God upon a people, any enterprise, house, village, town, city or nation, that is built on the slaughter of another people is under a woeful curse. For example: the somewhat present controversial, though now long dead British Methodist theologian, Adam Clarke, making reference to that great stink in some of our own nations at a particular time, and regarding the opening phrases of this verse comments saying:

Habakkuk 2:12-14

"Woe to him who builds a town with bloodshed, Who establishes a city by iniquity! Behold, is it not of the Lord of hosts That the peoples labor to feed the fire, And nations weary themselves in vain? For the earth will be filled With the knowledge of the glory of the Lord, As the waters cover the sea. NKJV

"And these things will refer to the vast fortunes gained, and the buildings erected, by means of the slave-trade; where, to a considerate and humane mind, the walls appear as if composed of the bones of negroes, and cemented by their blood! But the towns or houses established by this iniquity soon come to ruin; and the fortunes made have, in most cases, become as chaff and dust before the whirlwind of God's indignation. But where are the dealers in the souls and bodies of men? Ask him who has them in his keeping. He can tell."

Cruel oppression had been a blood red revenue stream into the coffers of Babylon since its foundation, and though since soon after the flood it had continued to aggrandize its edifices in magnificent wonder and seemingly strong and impenetrable defense, its inlaid walls were already rotting with the curse of peoples whose spilt, blood-squeezed sweat had built it and bound it all together in tears. Redeemed from the sands of time, a little of what is left of the burnt city of Babylon can be found in The British Museum in London, the greatest city of the western world. A little of what was good and is left of the British Empire, that first truly global superpower, can be seen in parliamentary democracy around the globe. However, just as Babylon disappeared beneath the sands, so did Britannia disappear beneath the waves of war, bankruptcy, colonial immigration and ultimately, in that experiment in 1/7th allotment of global control called the European Union. "Woe to him who builds a town with bloodshed, Who establishes a city by iniquity!"

Despite the seemingly unassailable protection of the riches of drug cartels, national mafias and all other unrighteous empires both large and small, no matter how many decades or centuries they seem to last, when built on the bloody backs of others, they shall fall and fall and fall.

There is a principle here: Despite the seemingly unassailable protection of the riches of drug cartels, national mafias and all other unrighteous empires both large and small, no matter how many decades or centuries they seem to last, when built on the bloody backs of others, they shall fall and fall and fall. So, tell me then tonight, are your little empires, your full, safe deposit boxes, your bank accounts, your self esteem, your prowess and prominence, your ego, are they all being built upon unrighteous foundations? Are their walls inlaid with the cursing of others who have wrongly been made less so that you could be made much more? I tell you now, if this is the case, whatever you have built, whoever you or your family are, both you and it, will not stand, no, you all shall fall and fall and fall.

Listen: *So they hanged Haman on the gallows that he had prepared for Mordecai. Then the king's wrath subsided. On that day King Ahasuerus gave Queen Esther the house of Haman, the enemy of the Jews. And Mordecai came before the king, for Esther had told how he was related to her. So the king took off his signet ring, which he had taken from Haman, and gave it to Mordecai; and Esther appointed Mordecai over the house of Haman. Esther 7:10-8:2 NKJV*

Pray: Lord, have mercy on our blushing lush, which at the expense of others, encases our feet in tight-fit trainers and covers our shoulders in sweat-shop cloth. Help us to live wisely and to live generously. Amen and let it be so.

Bible Insight 33

Woe three of five – The stoking of the Lord

T he artist spends months giving birth to his masterpiece and then lays it at the door of the furnace. The weaver, whose work of art is all interwoven with expensive gold coated wool with other strands dyed in the richest of colors, neatly rolls his years of laborious love up against the same hot furnace door. The sculptor sees the cart deliver up his beautiful bronze to the seven times heated fire and the architect, with the inside of his palm, brushes the marble walls, all inlaid with gold, as he is led away, inconsolable with tears of bitter grief. The great furnace doors are opened, and the stoker angels of the Most High God, faces like glistening alabaster in the white hot heat, begin to shovel all of these treasures into the open-mouth fires of retribution, breathing out the acid hot heat of righteous indignation. And though the artists and the architect, the historian and the preservation trustees, yes, though all the on-looking archeologists, investors, patrons and bankers are staring open-eyed through the dazed wonder of wasted years and the labor of their vanity, the fiery destruction is never the less, unstoppable, for this stoking is of The Lord.

Habakkuk 2:12-14

"Woe to him who builds a town with bloodshed, Who establishes a city by iniquity! Behold, is it not of the Lord of hosts That the peoples labor to feed the fire, And nations weary themselves in vain? For the earth will be filled With the knowledge of the glory of the Lord, As the waters cover the sea. NKJV

Here is truth: God's earth shall not be filled with the unrighteous regimes of man. Indeed, whatever nation, government or system, that is founded on unrighteous thievery for the purpose of self exaltation shall be burnt with fire. God cannot suffer it to be in His earth. Such so called 'glory of man', be it ever so great and fine, shall not be allowed to cover the earth of God. Therefore that nation, that empire that forgets God, expands and maintains, consolidates and embellishes, yes it labors in vein and shall ultimately fall. Yes indeed, even if that nation and empire once rose under God, and was established by the Lord, even if it's beautiful booty was as payment for being His judgment sword and His national assassin, yes even if that nation was once the apple of His eye, in its rich and arrogant forgetfulness it shall most surely fall.

The napalm of God is always dropped, yes, the flame thrower of God is always blasted and squirted against the base walls Babylon.

God takes no account of earthly prowess, nor of political power nor of manmade beauty. Such edifices which cannot exist accept without thievery, subjugation and unrighteousness, well, against such, the napalm of God is always dropped, yes, the flame thrower of God is always blasted and squirted against the base walls Babylon.

Be careful Christian for claiming that city in which you live for Jesus. Be careful Christian for such a dumb association and easy neighborliness with such foul unrighteousness. Be careful for seeking the peace and prosperity of that which is doomed, for there comes a point, where salt cannot preserve that which is already putrid, and where light can no longer shine in a black hole of unrighteous rebellion. Be careful Christian. Christian be wise. Maybe it is time to disengage? Maybe it is time to formulate an escape plan? Maybe it is time to pack your bags? Or maybe, you, Mrs Lot and the kids, have so sold out to your city and its pleasures, and have become so comfortable with the perversion, that and in all the overlooking you too have become blind to the brimstone ready to rain down upon your heads? Maybe it's time to go to 'Heaven's Son' and order some eye salve and a few suitcases?

Listen: *Babylon has suddenly fallen and been destroyed. Wail for her! Take balm for her pain; Perhaps she may be healed. We would have healed Babylon, But she is not healed. Forsake her, and let us go everyone to his own country; For her judgment reaches to heaven and is lifted up to the skies. Jeremiah 51:8-9 NKJV*

Thus says the Lord of hosts: "The broad walls of Babylon shall be utterly broken, And her high gates shall be burned with fire; The people will labor in vain, And the nations, because of the fire; And they shall be weary." Jeremiah 51:58 NKJV

Pray: O great God of the long time, give us mere 'May flies' a comforting view from your eternal vists tonight. Amen and let it be so.

Bible Insight 34

Woe three of five –The coming consolation of the planet

N ow we come to a most wonderful and most glorious emphatic statement which is the cuddling consolation of the weeping earth, whose atlas pillars have shouldered pig sties for far too many millennia. It is the song of the planets singing hope, for that time when earth shall become heaven:

Habakkuk 2:12-14

"Woe to him who builds a town with bloodshed, Who establishes a city by iniquity! Behold, is it not of the Lord of hosts That the peoples labor to feed the fire, And nations weary themselves in vain? For the earth will be filled With the knowledge of the glory of the Lord, As the waters cover the sea. NKJV

"For the earth will be filled With the knowledge of the glory of the Lord, As the waters cover the sea." NKJV

The comets of righteous judgments always leave a greater knowledge of God in their trail and just as Babylon past became forgotten ash and compost for the soil, so any future Babylon rising shall also become the same and so shall every institution, organization or nation which rejects and resists the right and might of God.

"For the earth will be filled With the knowledge of the glory of the Lord, As the waters cover the sea." NKJV

The Gospel will, can and must be spread to every tribe and tongue, yet it is not the good news of the grace of the King towards rebellious sinners which shall change the earth for good, no, but it is the very presence of the King of the Gospel which shall do that, and shall do it for a thousand years! When this happens, the knowledge of the glory of the Lord shall smooth out the jagged rocks of all unrighteousness and bury the radioactive stinkers in its all-consuming depths. When He comes to rule and reign, then the people shall walk upright once again and the stupefied shall become the sensible, the sleeping ignorant shall wake up wise, the wild and angry shall be flat calm happy, the hateful shall be lovable, yes, the hedonist shall become the selfless and even the mockers shall close their mouths and applaud in appreciation. In response, even nature herself with all her interwoven kingdoms, shall also change her clothes to smiling brightness and her manners along with them, giving up her rain in right measure, while the black panther which always walks by her side, shall only leave the dark forest to come and nuzzle the baby's head.

"For the earth will be filled With the knowledge of the glory of the Lord, As the waters cover the sea." NKJV

> *It is the church's job and privilege to proclaim her Master's grace across her Master's world but it is only the Master's arrival and the Master's presence which shall change the earth for good*

It is the church's job and privilege to proclaim her Master's grace across her Master's world but it is only the Master's arrival and the Master's presence which shall change the earth for good.

Listen: *"The wolf also shall dwell with the lamb, The leopard shall lie down with the young goat, The calf and the young lion and the fatling together; And a little child shall lead them. The cow and the bear shall graze; Their young ones shall lie down together; And the lion shall eat straw like the ox. The nursing child shall play by the cobra's hole, And the weaned child shall put his hand in the viper's den. They shall not hurt nor destroy in all My holy mountain, For the earth shall be full of the knowledge of the Lord As the waters cover the sea. Isaiah 11:6-9 NKJV*

Pray: Alpha and Omega, the beginning and the ending, You who are, and which was, and which is to come, the Almighty and everlasting Savior, come quickly. Amen and let it be so.

Bible Insight 35

Woe four of five – Demonic driven drug abuse

A drug culture is born from deliberate bondage. Get 'em hooked, keep 'em happy, keep 'em wanting more and keep 'em paying and when all the money runs out, have 'em steal it, have 'em sell their bodies and their very selves to the service of that which now enslaves them. And all the demons cry, "Strip them naked of any covering; rip off the covering clothes of any nobility, of any self respect and of any sensibility, yes let their shame be seen, yes, let us see these shaved and copulating monkey's dance themselves to death and so shall we cover the light of glory of this God with maggot infested shame."

Habakkuk 2:15-17

"Woe to him who gives drink to his neighbor, Pressing him to your bottle, Even to make him drunk, That you may look on his nakedness! You are filled with shame instead of glory. You also — drink! And be exposed as uncircumcised! The cup of the Lord's right hand will be turned against you, And utter shame will be on your glory. For the violence done to Lebanon will cover you, And the plunder of beasts which made them afraid, Because of men's blood And the violence of the land and the city, And of all who dwell in it. NKJV

Be it digested, injected or smoked, everything to do with drugs is rooted in the demonic and leads to idolatry, possession, loss, nakedness, shame and ultimate destruction.

Drug addiction is often encouraged. In this case there is reason to think that this imposed drunkenness also referred to the King of Egypt as the dealer in such pride who pressed the bottle of stupidity against the lips of Jehoiachin and Zedekiah to rebel against Nebuchadnezzar and that for the sole purpose of seeing them both stripped bare. There is something terribly perverted and devilishly pornographic in setting people up for such shameful destruction and to be so pleased by it. Fair words which cover foul deeds are the filth which shall later be spewed up. So watch now! Do you really think you shall make yourself great by bringing others down? You shall not, for there is always a curse in such mocking of an individual or even a nation's drunken nakedness, especially if you were the part cause of it. Indeed, such perverted people shall themselves become satiated with shame and full of a nose-pinching revolting loathsomeness, as they lie there, overwhelmed with their vomiting greed and the nations of Nuremburg spit their contempt on the scuffed boots of the remaining henchmen which now swing on the judgment gallows. "You are filled with shame instead of glory."

Understand this: Such perverted drunkenness was all-indulging and all-consuming, such that the trees of the forest of Lebanon were wastefully destroyed and the animals slaughtered to near extinction.

When a nation seeks to prosper on the greedy, hedonistic, selfish and unsustainable self-indulgence of its own citizens, then it will itself be eventually found in a damp field, covered in its own vomit, having spewed up all it had once taken in, its pants around its ankles and its buttocks laid bare to the laughing skies

All demonic drug culture is indulgent and ultimately all-consuming. When a nation seeks to prosper on the greedy, hedonistic, selfish and unsustainable self-indulgence of its own citizens, then it will itself be eventually found in a damp field, covered in its own vomit, having spewed up all it had once taken in, its pants around its ankles and its buttocks laid bare to the laughing skies.

Christian. You cannot be involved in the demonic activities of drunkenness and drugs and still call yourself by the name of Christ. Repent of this great evil. Get out, get sober, get clean. Get yourself sorted out!

Listen: *For thus says the Lord God of Israel to me: "Take this wine cup of fury from My hand, and cause all the nations, to whom I send you, to drink it. And they will drink and stagger and go mad because of the sword that I will send among them." Then I took the cup from the Lord's hand, and made all the nations drink, to whom the Lord had sent me: Jeremiah 25:15-17 NKJV*

Pray: Lord, be our consolation and our comfort, our joy and our exaltation, our stability and our peace. Amen and let it be so.

Bible Insight 36

Woe five of five – The idolatry of being spiritual

Drunkeness and drug culture, selfish destructive hedonism will always lead to the substitution of the creator God with the stupidity of idolatry. Demons, clothing themselves in the clothes of post modern plurality, display themselves openly in shop windows alongside all the bonging paraphernalia of bondage, for when people reject belief in the God of the Bible, they believe anything.

Habakkuk 2:18,19

"What profit is the image, that its maker should carve it, The molded image, a teacher of lies, That the maker of its mold should trust in it, To make mute idols? Woe to him who says to wood, 'Awake!' To silent stone, 'Arise! It shall teach!' Behold, it is overlaid with gold and silver, Yet in it there is no breath at all. NKJV

There is no breath, that is, there is no life in any demonic inspired man-made religion. Even if that religion is overlaid with gold and silver and rooted in the organic, it has no creating voice, it cannot speak, it cannot call for the life and light and love. It is dead and any animation you find is merely the demonic clothed in a raincoat and wearing a mask. mumbling lies and fiddling with your children as you place them on its knees and sit them in its fiery arms.

Tell me. What is the end of such ignorant idolatry, such demonic and drunken bondage?

Listen: *Professing to be wise, they became fools, and changed the glory of the incorruptible God into an image made like corruptible man — and birds and four-footed animals and creeping things. Therefore God also gave them up to uncleanness, in the lusts of their hearts, to dishonor their bodies among themselves, who exchanged the truth of God for the lie, and worshiped and served the creature rather than the Creator, who is blessed forever. Amen. For this reason God gave them up to vile passions. For even their women exchanged the natural use for what is against nature. Likewise also the men, leaving the natural use of the woman, burned in their lust for one another, men with men committing what is shameful, and receiving in themselves the penalty of their error which was due. And even as they did not like to retain God in their knowledge, God gave them over to a debased mind, to do those things which are not fitting; being filled with all unrighteousness, sexual immorality, wickedness, covetousness, maliciousness; full of envy, murder, strife, deceit, evil-mindedness; they are whisperers, backbiters, haters of God, violent, proud, boasters, inventors of evil things, disobedient to parents, undiscerning, untrustworthy, unloving, unforgiving, unmerciful; who, knowing the righteous judgment of God, that those who practice such things are deserving of death, not only do the same but also approve of those who practice them. Romans 1:22-32NKJV*

Pray: Let the knowledge of the Lord be in our mouths and upon our lips, let all the unrighteous airwaves dance with it and let it fill the ears of the deaf. Amen and let it be so.

Bible Insight 37

Sorted and therefore settled peace

The just shall live by faith in the great fact that the glory of the Lord shall one day cover the earth and we are now assured of this in this verse and subsequently commanded to quietness before the Lord's sage and sovereign government. God is in control. God is on the only throne that matters, the holy throne of His temple and it is only a vision of this total sovereignty of God that will turn our watching souls from worry to worship, and from spluttering and stuttering panic to a deep breathing and quiet peace; a hushness of holiness in His steady and ruling presence.

Habakkuk 2: 20

"But the Lord is in His holy temple. Let all the earth keep silence before Him." NKJV

Solomon, the builder of the first earthly temple clearly declared that the heavens and even the heaven of heavens cannot contain the fullness of God (1 Kings 8:27), yet God is everywhere, all at once, at the same time, in whom we live and move and have our being, while manifesting Himself in the Shekinah glory of the mercy seat above the ark and also in the two-legged temple of His only begotten Son, Jesus Christ our Lord is also localized in His temple in heaven. In this way, God is never absent from His throne of ruling dominion. He is always at the wheel, at the helm, at the desk, in the only 'Oval Office' that matters.

Christian, you may think that God is doing a bad job in His governing of the nations, but it is His job never the less. Trust Him to bring forth good. Stop your judging of God! Who are you, you mere lump of mouthy clay? Stop whining, stop worrying, stop complaining! Humble yourself, get on your face and worship Him. Be quiet. Hush. Be still. The Lord reigns, yes, even now in your life, in your city, in your nation, the Lord still reigns from the supreme place of government, His holy temple. He has not left there. He has not taken a holiday or gone on a golfing trip. The Lord is reigning still.

Faith in the sovereignty of God, based on the solid declarations of His government, will lead to stillness and eventually to singing. As for Habakkuk, a sonata will now follow this humbled silence of the prophet as he himself leads the world in silent and bowing obeisance. Take Psalm 11 right now and make it your singing prayer tonight.

Listen: *In the Lord I put my trust; How can you say to my soul, "Flee as a bird to your mountain" For look! The wicked bend their bow, They make ready their arrow on the string, That they may shoot secretly at the upright in heart. If the foundations are destroyed, What can the righteous do? The Lord is in His holy temple, The Lord's throne is in heaven; His eyes behold, His eyelids test the sons of men. The Lord tests the righteous, But the wicked and the one who loves violence His soul hates. Upon the wicked He will rain coals; Fire and brimstone and a burning wind Shall be the portion of their cup. For the Lord is righteous, He loves righteousness; His countenance beholds the upright. Psalms 11 NKJV*

Pray: Settled are we O Lord on You and Your sovereign will. Gracious Sovereign, come and be ruler of my own heart and mind and mouth. Amen and may I always praise Your holy name.

Bible Insight 38

The dithyrambic destruction of despair, doubt and depression

It has been said that "If you want to get out from under a load, then you must get under the Lord!" Habakkuk chose to get under the Lord, and to believe that God was greater than his circumstances. This 'Shigionoth,' is probably a very much devised and specific form of battle praise, which in turn, is rooted in the revelation of God, and is a purposefully upbeat, rhythmic, exuberant and even wild declaration of faith, which is slapped down like a gauntlet across the face of all that is contrary to joy, to peace, to prosperity and to happiness. Shigionoth then, is a planned attack on fear, it is a dithyrambic destruction of doubt, despondency and depression! It is a neck-bracing, eye-lifting, 'get up of your whining backside and look at our Great Lord', lifter- up of the heart kind of singing! It is a coagulation of different meandering voices and wandering words, a collection of choral dithyrambics, all couched in symphonic surround sound of stringed instruments, and with instructions for the director of music in Habakkuk 3:19, this mad song of stunning victory is a public cacophony of praise to be sung in the presence of the waiting and the worshipping people of God.

Habakkuk 3:1

*A prayer of Habakkuk
the prophet upon
Shigionoth. KJV*

Now, I am labouring the wonder of this prophetic construction of choral praise set to multi- stringed accompaniment, to emphasize that, though sometimes the clouds of heaviness are seemingly parted directly by both the out turned palms of God, more often than not however, such a parting of the covering of the dark clouds of depression, despondency doubt, fear and a thousand other foul atmospheres of hell, are in fact carried out by the raised palms of our own hands of praise. Faith, you see, is an exercise of the voice, yes, hope that brings peace is a tune of the well learned song, and the perfume of a well constructed and communal expression of unified belief. In other words dear friends, more often than not, we have to come up with our own song to sing ourselves out from under a load and place ourselves under the Lord!

Now, may I say that this should encourage us! It is in our power to look out of the dark cave of Adullam, and even in the earthquake, wind and fire of our days, to come to the mouth of our Horeb hideaway and sing in the sunshine of the greatness and the goodness of God. Some of us tonight then don't need to find a new song to sing, we need to write one!

Listen: *Why are you cast down, O my soul? And why are you disquieted within me? Hope in God, for I shall yet praise Him For the help of His countenance. Psalms 42:5 NKJV*

Pray: O Lord my God, in You I put my trust; Save me from all those who persecute me; And deliver me, Lest they tear me like a lion, Rending me in pieces, while there is none to deliver. O Lord my God, if I have done this: If there is iniquity in my hands, If I have repaid evil to him who was at peace with me, Or have plundered my enemy without cause, Let the enemy pursue me and overtake me; Yes, let him trample my life to the earth, And lay my honor in the dust. Selah? (Psalm 7:1-5 - Prayer and Praise for Deliverance from Enemies A Shigionoth of David, which he sang to the Lord concerning the words of Cush, a Benjamite.)

Bible Insight 39

Real revival and the custard pie cannon of the man on the moon

This verse is the essence and the core of the prayer of the prophet, and in being so, it is the striking chord of all the verses of battle praise to follow.

Habakkuk 3:2

O Lord, I have heard Your speech and was afraid; O Lord, revive Your work in the midst of the years! In the midst of the years make it known; In wrath remember mercy. NKJV

Publicly, in front of maybe around 200 senior Pastors, the 'prophet' called me to the front of the gathering and began proclaiming the great things that God was going to do in and through me. It was unexpected. It was great. Yes, it was an honor to be so publicly honored! I eventually returned to my seat to WOWS, embraces and back-slapping welcomes. As the gathered power house of Pastors then turned to other business the bearded man in the row in front, quietly turned to me with an open Bible, pointed to a particular text, and said: "I feel the Lord wants you to know this as well." I believe it was Acts 9:16 which read: "For I will show him how many things he must suffer for My name's sake." Frankly, like long hung curtains in sunshine windows, everything of color preceding this became quickly faded, dusty and limp, for friends, what is the chaff compared to the wheat? The more real Word of the Lord had come and it had been banged with force on the door of my 'knower', yes, "I had heard His speech and I was afraid." It seemed as though 'this word' was the summary side product of the whole previous report.

Habakkuk was in an awful state. He was full of awe, that long lost mixture of trembling fear, holy dread, wonder and broken hearted worship, which is now hardly ever seen in the modern church. His prayer from this awful position which he found himself in, was still based on the mercy of God, for though he knew the well deserved and terrible judgment that was coming, yes, though he had seen it all in terrible Technicolor, he now moved himself under God and got himself a greater vision of God's greater and ever perfect and overall work, and from here, began to involve himself in that, even seemingly acting like Abraham, when he bargained and bartered for His nephew Lot who was residing in Sodom before the fire and brimstone fell. So Habakkuk also prayerfully tries to pluck some triple goodness out of the fire of God's present judgment.

1) "O Lord, revive Your work in the midst of the years! 2) In the midst of the years make it known; 3) In wrath remember mercy."

"O Lord, revive Your work in the midst of the years!" Yes, in the middle of the mess Lord, revive Your work. Not our dead works which have failed to steer us from riding over the edge of this cliff of national disaster, but Your long inactive work, that great Gospel work of the Holy Spirit, which, like the long dead winter

Only a 'back to the Bible' revolution will put the people of God back under the greatness of God.

trees, is presently cold, brittle, leafless and dead in the land of the hungry lumberjack. Revive that Lord! In the middle of this age of ice and cold, dead hearts, do a miracle here. Adjust the atmosphere here. Arrange the stars for us here. Make us the pinnacle of this planet and then tilt our spinning globe toward the warmth of Your life-giving rays. Melt the ice around us. Wake up the trees! Bring forth the bud, the flower and the fruit. In the middle of winter, let there be a revival of the repentant, yes, in wrath O Lord, please remember mercy.

As I write this Bible insight in 2014, the USA, like a wise Judah, in awful dread observes the overrunning of the Israel of God across 'the pond', and shakes her head at the state of the work of the Lord in these islands. 'Over there' that is, among us here, even that oft trumped promise of a 'prophesied' coming revival, sounds more like the hope of the indiscriminate firing at the earth, of a custard pie cannon from a deranged man on the moon. As one UK Christian leader may have put it: revival may splat us here, or there, who knows! Maybe tomorrow or maybe on a Thursday in 2025 in Scotland. But sometime, somewhere, the mad man on the moon will fire the custard pie revival canon and when it splats the earth, then all be well, yes, things will never be the same again! The tide will turn and all our problems and persecutions will turn to treacle. Friends, this is vain hope and I tell you now, it is not Habakkuk's hope. "In Your wrath, remember mercy."

Only a 'back to the Bible' revolution will put the people of God back under the greatness of God. Only from here shall we see the larger and more perfect work of God. Only from here shall we be able to truly pray and prepare for a revival of mercy in the middle of wrath, for a warming in the winter, for the central trees of the forest to be touched with life while the outer ones are cut down around them and burned in the fire! It is in the middle of it 'all', you see, that we can and must pray for a revival of God's work. Even so, and do not forget this, even so Sodom, and Jerusalem which has become like Sodom, shall still be set aflame.

He who has ears to hear. Let him hear.

Listen: *We have heard with our ears, O God, Our fathers have told us, The deeds You did in their days, In days of old: You drove out the nations with Your hand, But them You planted; You afflicted the peoples, and cast them out. For they did not gain possession of the land by their own sword, Nor did their own arm save them; But it was Your right hand, Your arm, and the light of Your countenance, Because You favored them. You are my King, O God; Command victories for Jacob. Psalms 44:1-4 NKJV*

Pray: We are valuable O Lord. However, we acknowledge that we are not indispensible. Therefore, O Great King of ages, in Your wrath remember mercy, and in the middle of this increasing disaster, revive Your work O Lord. Amen and let it be so.

Bible Insight 40

Lighting the blue touch paper

I like to imagine this great symphonic and choral work of chapter three being performed in three major parts and this being the beginning or part two. I imagine a solitary Temple singer standing and powerfully proclaiming the words: "God came from Teman, The Holy One from Mount Paran." and in the following semi-silence that such a powerful invocation of common cultural covenant history of the redeemed people of God intends to invoke, the pause of the Selah allowed the mass choirs to stand and the 'orchestra' to prepare their joint explosive entrance which would follow that invoked pause. In Britain, domestic fireworks have always had paper fuses impregnated with 'salt-peter' and dyed blue. The instructions for use have invariable been as follows: "Light the blue touch paper and immediately retire." In other words, light the fuse, stand well back and watch the fire work! Here, in this covenant and cultural invocation, Habakkuk has lit the blue touch paper. Stand well back now!

Habakkuk 3:3

God came from Teman, The Holy One from Mount Paran. Selah His glory covered the heavens, And the earth was full of His praise. NKJV

However, before all the sky filling explosions of glittering colors, let us briefly enter the same covenant pause. "God came from Teman, The Holy One from Mount Paran. Selah." If you were a Jew, who from birth had been steeped in the story of the Exodus and annually celebrated the Passover, then such Biblically poetic imagery, even in this brief moment of time, would have embraced, enveloped and gathered up that march of Israel from the Sinai Peninsula to the Promised Land. I wonder if forty years of wandering and wonder, of judgment and joy, of manna and miracle, of pillar, presence and preparation, might have been gathered in a pause of less than four seconds? After all, we that are older both know and appreciate that years of study and a life time of understanding can come together in just a few moments of meditation. Remember that. Selah.

I wonder that if when God comes to you and says "Remember", yes, when in your spirit the Holy Spirit has lit your own blue touch paper, then it might be wise to "retire immediately", yes, to "stand well back" even, for maybe God is about to explode a few chrysanthemum mortar rockets of His own across the dark skies of your present understanding, and in the coming flare of His own firework favor toward you, the unseen faith paths below you, hesitant and fearful, shall be revealed enough to you, that the way into the Promised Land shall be clearly unveiled as existent, definite, real and walkable.

> *God intends to do You good and to bring you to places of His promises. So then dear friend, press on!*

Christian! Mark well the past mercies of Your God in deliverances now long gone. Note well His ever presence and be assured of the promise of His continuous guidance. God intends to do You good and to bring you to places of His promises. So then dear friend, press on!

Listen: *Now this is the blessing with which Moses the man of God blessed the children of Israel before his death. And he said: "The Lord came from Sinai, And dawned on them from Seir; He shone forth from Mount Paran, And He came with ten thousands of saints; From His right hand Came a fiery law for them. Yes, He loves the people; All His saints are in Your hand; They sit down at Your feet; everyone receives Your words. Deuteronomy 33:1-3 NKJV*

Pray: Father we look to the night skies of our own being. Father, we look to the external skies of your past providences and our present circumstances. In explosive wonder O Lord, and drape your glittering goodness and starlight our way in color glorious, that we, in pursuit of your will for our life, might continue to please You as we are encouraged to press on in our walk of faith with You. Amen and let it be so.

Bible Insight 41

Look to the skies!

In the light of the coming wrath, underneath the umbrella of God's mercy toward the remnant, Habakkuk now invokes the covenant community, cultural remembrance of the Exodus manifestation of the Most High in power-packed and poetical imagery. He desires for them in both symphonic sound and choral song, to have this powerful redemptive picture embossed on the frontal lobes of all their own soon coming wanderings and displacements. He wants them to see the cloudy and the fiery pillar, come and brand their own current dry and cow hide earth with His personal ownership of all the on-coming trouble. Today, every roaming remnant, and every remaining tree stub, both need to remember the glorious and ruling power of God, for without this, the noon day of God's wrath would quickly curl any green hope of present mercy and bud of future goodness into a dark brown dead and crispy leaf, easily crumpled into dust under a marching Babylonian boot. In your present troubles then my friend, remember the former outward manifestation of the greatness of God in your life. Remember.

Habakkuk 3:3

God came from Teman, The Holy One from Mount Paran. Selah His glory covered the heavens, And the earth was full of His praise. NKJV

In each twenty four hour cycle, daily light decks the black, star freckled, cold and waiting skies, in the triple walking wonders of sunrise glory, daffodil noon day highs, and the rich red and soft seductive hues of evenings, all waiting with smiles and open, cotton bedclothes, cocooning silk and soft skinned wives. Look up! For His glory always covers the heavens.

In particular, however, remember that when God came from Teman, yes, when the Holy One came to His people from Mount Paran, below, the earth sizzled with the scorch marks of His pillared and fiery stepping paw, and above, the heavens hummed with His power plant presence, whilst the cumulus clouds revolved in reflective metallic rainbow colors, all the while bowing in a perpetual self -enfolding obeisance to God's presence in the skies, yes, even soiling themselves in rained out awe, as His molten 'magic' tripped the light fantastic in disco flashing surprise.

That time, do you remember, that time when your chest beat in boom box unison with the booming heart of God. Think back now. Think back and remember?

In your life right now then, look up! The glory of God is still daily present. But do not forget those other special days long gone, no, call them to mind and suck on those previous times of awe, when in those special seasons of your past, God was unexpectedly found in the sober tent of the vineyard of His goodness, and was there seen unclothed to you, revealing just a little of His glory, yes, just enough to leave you breathless in watching wonder, eager in anticipation, and dreamy in the delightful consummation of His kindness and His waiting will for you. Remember?

Friend, in the coming wanderings, and in all the now black rumblings above the wide umbrella of His mercy, yes, even amidst the cold dark downpour going on around you, huddle down and remember, yes, call to mind the wonders of His previous visitations of you.

Friend, in the coming wanderings, and in all the now black rumblings above the wide umbrella of His mercy, yes, even amidst the cold dark downpour going on around you, huddle down and remember, yes, call to mind the wonders of His previous visitations of you, those particular times of your past, when His heavenly glory once touched Your once forgotten and unexpected days. Look now! Even this storm of wrath shall pass and soon and very soon as well! For the earth shall be filled with the knowledge of the glory of the LORD as the waters cover the sea, and yes, you shall be there to see it.

Remember this.

Listen: *"O Job; Stand still and consider the wondrous works of God. Do you know when God dispatches them, And causes the light of His cloud to shine? Do you know how the clouds are balanced, those wondrous works of Him who is perfect in knowledge? Why are your garments hot, when He quiets the earth by the south wind? With Him, have you spread out the skies, Strong as a cast metal mirror? "Teach us what we should say to Him, For we can prepare nothing because of the darkness. Should He be told that I wish to speak? If a man were to* *speak, surely he would be swallowed up. Even now men cannot look at the light when it is bright in the skies, When the wind has passed and cleared them. He comes from the north as golden splendor; With God is awesome majesty. Job 37:14-22 NKJV*

Pray: Father, help me recall the former days of Your goodness, that in my present distresses, my courage would not fail. Father, help me recall the ever present promises of all Your future goodness, that in my present distresses. my hope would never die. So make me live, and make my eyes reflect Your glory. So make me live, and set the display of my countenance to ever be a picture of Your greatness and Your hidden all sufficiency. Amen and let it be so.

Bible Insight 42

The hymn of the earth to the Him on the earth

"And the earth was full of His praise."

Quite literally here, the arrival of the risen up Lord of Exodus redemption, in His fiery pillar intrusion into His space-time continuum, hit several notes with planet earth, and so much so, that the earth was multiplied with the laudations of their Creator's magnificent presence.

Habakkuk 3:3

God came from Teman,
The Holy One from
Mount Paran. Selah. His
glory covered the
heavens, and the earth
was full of His praise.
NKJV

In the wilderness the fiery pillar scorched the sand, and all the brother silicates, sucked in their breath and sang out with the rest of the reverberating earth, a pulsating praise to the testimony of His presence.

Every part of creation is animate in the sight of the Lord, is purposeful in His pre-shaping hands, is molded, measured, tested, utilized and known by Him. All matter 'lives,' you see, and has a life that is meaningful and pleasant to its Creator and together with the rest of matter, sings its Creators praises while groaning out its present desire for deliverance from the bondage and curse of sin. All things live to Him who created them and praise Him in the uniqueness of their distinct created voice. In addition to this, all things have a desire to be what they were destined for, to be what they were created to be and when this cannot be achieved, then they groan in creaking misplacement against the cruel shapes they have been made to conform to, against the dullness that has robbed them of their sheen, against the black spider cracks of the now tarnished silvered God reflecting mirror. Nothing of matter is truly dead you see, indeed, when "the earth shall be filled with the knowledge of the glory of the Lord as the waters cover the sea", then creation itself will come alive like a resurrected Eden. Yes, in more solid color, in fantastic fragrance, in sound perceptible, and ways currently inconceivable, all things shall then manifest their true nature, yes, the lion shall lie down with the lamb and even the dessert shall bloom when the Lord of the earth comes in unwrapped glory to rule the footstool of His love. Look now! When the Father last intruded into the space time continuum, the earth was full of His praise!

All the purifying fires of God, shall simply make His treasure shine all the more. So, tell me now dear Christian then, does Christ in You the hope of glory make your whole being sing and shine? Is every part of you touched with the praises of God tonight? No. I did not think so. Indeed, how quiet sometime is the regenerate being. How dull of heart and blind of eye, how bereft of any song are those whose praise should reach the sky? I am ashamed to say that I stand with you tonight in this travesty of a testimony to the presence of Christ in us, and the ignorance of the words of our own new song of redemptive praise. The current deceptions of the devil, still run deep in us do they not, and still blinker our vision to the ministering angels which daily attend our way?

We who have the earnest of the Spirit have become dissatisfied in the waiting for the Glories of son-ship to come and so in the mean time, have chosen the worship of idols.

I have two things for your consideration this day.

Maybe tonight we need to ask God to manifest His presence within us, and touch Himself down with fire in the inner wilderness of our being, so that our own dessert would start to sing once more and the earth of our own being would at last be full of His praises. Ask Him.

More likely though, we have given our heart away to another. Unlike the earth, still praising in travail and groaning for the adoption, we who have the earnest of the Spirit have become dissatisfied in the waiting for the Glories of son-ship to come and so in the mean time, have chosen the worship of idols. In the bed of your heart my unpraising brother, my silly sister lies something or someone else other than your Lord. I guarantee it. Now then, throw it out! Give it its divorce papers and send it back to Egypt. Clean house and make room for your God once more, you wicked and adulterous individual. This is the problem and there is no excuse for it.

Repent first, then child of God, you might just begin to rejoice evermore.

Listen: *"Hear, O kings! Give ear, O princes! I, even I, will sing to the Lord; I will sing praise to the Lord God of Israel. Lord, when You went* *out from Seir, when You marched from the field of Edom, the earth trembled and the heavens poured, the clouds also poured water; The mountains gushed before the Lord, this Sinai, before the Lord God of Israel. Judges 5:3-5 NKJV*

Pray: So the tears of our repentance pour forth now O God as we ask forgiveness for our idolatry. Now then, O great Father, would you stir Yourself is us once more, would you come and touch the earth of our being that we would rightly reverberate in praise to You O Most High God. Amen and let it be so.

Bible Insight 43

God's ray guns

So now, Habakkuk continues his calling to the mind of his hearers, that arrival of the risen up Lord of the Exodus redemption and His fiery pillar intrusion into His space-time continuum. The fact that this manifestation of God had a physical impact upon the physical world had a two-fold witness. First, that His power was most clearly seen in the manifestation of His laser-like blasting hands, for from His open hands it was not mere glittering sparklers that effervesced out of His open palms, but rather, it was hard bolts of high voltage power that zigzagged explosively across the ground, and danced upon the rocks, and whatever other bulls-eye target He so desired to disintegrate! Yes, this was more than a Catherine Wheel collection of warm sunshine rays illuminating from, and radiating out of God's 'wax on-wax off' hands, for out of His palms came quite literally 'horns' of sharp, white flashing power.

Habakkuk 3:4

His brightness was like the light; He had rays flashing from His hand, and there His power was hidden. NKJV

Secondly, the atmosphere around the exploding presence was also severely affected, such that cumulus steam clouds and torrents of rain poured down like power showers around the moving manifestation of this powerful and fiery pillar. Because of the elemental response to the pillars presence, this manifestation of God could remain mostly hidden and covered, masked and blurred, with any image or person of the Godhead contained therein, all suitably clothed in clouds and hidden in a hooded habit, woven with water flashing, splashing splendor. In these two things, His power was most clearly seen and the yet the cause of it was most clearly hidden.

In far gentler ways of wonder, some 2,000 years ago, this same God was manifest in the walking mercy seat of His Son our Savior, Jesus Christ the Lord. The Shekinah glory in all its enfolding pulsating power enveloped the core of Jesus' dark badger-skinned covered, internal being whilst around His feet poured out tears of sorrow for lost humanity. The mount of transfiguration and the weeping wailing outside the tomb of Lazarus, showed great glimpses in the lifting of the hem of His garment in these two things, for Christ came then in His humility and not in His manifest glory.

Though Ananias and his wife Sapphira might disagree, the present manifestations of the power of His hands are still mostly the gentle coruscations of warm, moth drawing light. Presently as well, in the manifestation of His presence, God and even His mighty ministering angels, still often choose, it would seem, to wear some disguises, though for sure, they are much more subtle: A gardener, a disappearing lunch guest, men on a mission in need of a roof and food and a bed for the night. Angels unawares!

In the redeeming of people who have seen the light, God reveals His power. In glimpses and disguise, God still presently hides the same. For now

In the redeeming of people who have seen the light, God reveals His power. In glimpses and disguise, God still presently hides the same. For now.

Meanwhile, these Habakkuk verses tonight, remind us that if God wants to get out His ray gun, He can!

Listen: *Now it came to pass, as He sat at the table with them, that He took bread, blessed and broke it, and gave it to them. Then their eyes were opened and they knew Him; and He vanished from their sight. And they said to one another, "Did not our heart burn within us while He talked with us on the road, and while He opened the Scriptures to us?" Luke 24:30-32 NKJV*

Pray: Father, hide not from me! O Lord, reveal yourself to dullard me. God I desire to see You and if not that, to at least see Your works and hear you walking in my garden. God reveal Yourself to me. Amen and let it be so.

Bible Insight 44

The only 'Plague-arism' to be truly concerned about

Of course this pestilence referred directly to the plagues laid upon the backs of the Egyptians who held Israel in bondage for four hundred years. However, more than that, the same judgment has been used by God against many an army and people that might try and resist His will, even His own people Israel. Indeed, pestilence is that speedy visitation of an unusually rapid and advancing vicious and voracious killing disease, which destroys the larger percentages of the very quickly stricken. Death within hours and death to exceptionally large quantities of those infected.

Habakkuk 3:5

Before Him went pestilence, And fever followed at His feet.
NKJV

Here the primary disseminator of such disease is neither the flea nor the rat, nor the dank air, nor the foul infected water, but God Himself; His hot coaled feet driving the plague before Him and leaving brow beating fevers behind Him. This pestilent plaguing is a biological agent of the judgment of God, the slashing of which has repeatedly dispatched people in their tens of thousands at a time. In this respect, burning fever and pestilent death are the vanguards of the marching of the Lord. Remember, God is awful and to those who might try and resist Him, He is terrifying.

This Gospel dispensation in which we stand is truly one of blood bought grace. The first miracle wrought and delivered by the hand of Moses upon the Egyptians was the turning of water into blood. The first miracle of the Son of God was the turning of water in rich red wine. The new covenant moves us from pestilence to party.

The context of Chapter 3:5 of course is that Habakkuk is reminding the people to remember the incredible fierceness of their God when compared to the fierceness of the coming Chaldeans. What God has done against His enemies in the past, He can do to His enemies in the future. In this, they needed to take courage and so my friends do we.

Times of trouble are coming upon us and we need to remember that should He so wish, God can take care of those who trouble us very quickly indeed.

Listen: *He who dwells in the secret place of the Most High Shall abide under the shadow of the Almighty. I will say of the Lord, "He is my refuge and my fortress; My God, in Him I will trust." Surely He shall deliver you from the snare of the fowler And from the perilous pestilence. He shall cover you with His feathers, And under His wings you shall take refuge; His truth shall be your shield and buckler. You shall not be afraid of the terror by night, Nor of the arrow that flies by day, Nor of the pestilence that walks in darkness, Nor of the destruction that lays waste at noonday. A thousand may fall at your side, And ten thousand at your right hand; But it shall not come near you. Only with your eyes shall you look, And see the reward of the wicked. Psalms 91:1-8 NKJV*

Pray: I have made You O Lord my refuge, and You Most High, my dwelling place. Therefore let no evil shall befall me, nor any plague come near my dwelling; Give Your angels charge over me and keep me safe and certain in all my ways, let them guide me and bear me up lest I dash my foot against a stone. So shall I tread upon the lion and the cobra, the young lion and the serpent shall be trampled beneath my feet for You have set Your love upon me to deliver me; and set me on high, because he O know and am known by Your name O Lord of Hosts. I call upon you in the day of trouble; so deliver me and honor me O God, and with long life satisfy me and show me Your salvation. Amen and let it be so.

Bible Insight 45

Well hard!

He stood; He looked; He startled; He scattered. He bent;

When God stands up, everyone else had better sit down. When God stands up it is to do judgment business, and He does it openly, and conspicuously, yes, there is no disguise here in the standing of the Lord, for this is His own very personal act of His own Sovereign business. Be sure of this: When God stands up, He shall only sit down again in accomplished purpose and victory.

Habakkuk 3:6

He stood and measured the earth; He looked and startled the nations. And the everlasting mountains were scattered, The perpetual hills bowed. His ways are everlasting. NKJV

So God stands, wheels out His measuring tape and stretches Himself across the land, arms outstretched from East to West, from North to South. He stands for the very purpose of dividing the earth up and in particular to give the promised land to His people Israel and in further subdivision to each tribe and then intricately apportion a section of to each family therein. God knows each portion of property, earthly, heavenly, or otherwise, that He is, with sovereign benefice, granting to His people. "The earth is the Lord's," remember that, "and the fullness thereof."

So when God stood, He looked and the people and nations on the other end of that stare were startled! Quite literally, He gave them such a fright with His eyes that the nations leapt, like a flea from the scratch of the big dog in His own back yard, yes, their bursting heart thrust itself through their chest like a big base drum banging cartoon, whilst their eyes popped out of their head on stalks and their lower jaw dropped, port-cullies like, exploding in iron shattering fear to the ground. Note this now, when nations know that it is with a standing Lord they have to do, then they fear, yes, they quake, for like a bull in a Babylonian China shop, God shall scatter them in pieces across the face of the earth.

The perpetual hill bowed down. Those seemingly fixed edifices of indestructible and immense immovability were smashed into base little rocks across the iron face of the down swinging sledgehammer of God! Then, ground into fine power, they were thrown dust toward the four winds of the earth and consumed in passing time. Humanity has enough of its own history to know just how mountainous empires have long since gone, not least we the British.

Remember tonight then, that God's power is undiminished, unfaded, steady, strong and true and even now, He upholds all things by the word of His power.

In contrast dear reader, God's ways are everlasting, it is the same word translated 'perpetual' here, accept there is no crumbling in its associated longevity, no wearing, no eroding, no moving out of place. What we consider to be 'everlasting' are but a few ticks across the clock-face of God! God's ways, however, are truly everlasting.

Remember tonight then, that God's power is undiminished, unfaded, steady, strong and true and even now, He upholds all things by the word of His power. His measure and plan reached back into eternity, stretched wide across infinite possibility and lengthened long into a secure and future certainty for you. Saint of the most High God! God shall stand for You as well!

Listen: *Which of the prophets did your fathers not persecute? And they killed those who foretold the coming of the Just One, of whom you now have become the betrayers and murderers, who have received the law by the direction of angels and have not kept it." When they heard these things they were cut to the heart, and they gnashed at him with their teeth. But he, being full of the Holy Spirit, gazed into heaven and saw the glory of God, and Jesus standing at the right hand of God, and said, "Look! I see the heavens opened and the Son of Man standing at the right hand of God!" Acts 7:52-56 NKJV*

Pray: Stand O Lord for me and plead my cause amongst the liars and the unrighteous. Stand for me O God and protect me for my enemies. Stand for me O God as I stand for You and receive me into Your glory. So strengthen me for my death and glorious entrance into heaven. Amen and let it be so.

Bible Insight 46

Of the battalion flood and charging waters

At the time of my writing, I am on the protected harbor quayside of the bay of Kirkcaldy looking out at right angles across the watery expanse of the Firth of Forth to Arthur's seat upon the heights of the city of Edinburgh. The incoming tide, like white feathered charging cavalry, daily and continually roll and rush past my window to break themselves in victory upon the well beaten, salt waves eaten, broken down old sea wall. Ah, and when the big waves rise out of these seas, it is as though God raises His very self out of the boiling waters and then stands astride these rolling and frothing mounts, whilst screaming aloud in joyous victory as He guides the chariot charging waters all on their wall stampeding course. God is not angry at nature, but rather, He uses the great forces of nature to fulfill both His judgment and His redemptive purposes.

Habakkuk 3:7-9

I saw the tents of Cushan in affliction; The curtains of the land of Midian trembled. O Lord, were You displeased with the rivers, Was Your anger against the rivers, Was Your wrath against the sea, That You rode on Your horses, Your chariots of salvation? Your bow was made quite ready; Oaths were sworn over Your arrows. Selah NKJV

Now, from afar, Habakkuk speaks of the judgment of God as He now, in full and open display, removes His bow from its protective casing. In front of all resistive nations, here God 'unsheaths' His weapon, yes, He 'unholsters' His snipers rifle, and reaches to the rear of His right shoulder to pull from the prepared and well stocked quiver, the arrows of His promises, all inscribed down the shaft, even from flight to arrow head, with the sure oaths of His purpose and the covenants of His judgment and deliverance, both of which are certain.

For Judah there is a picture here, for at any time, at the right time, in His time, the seas shall be drawn back and the rivers shall part, as He in person flies with the swiftness of an unturned arrow, to land dead centre on the mark of His judgment and the point of His deliverance. For you dear reader, there is also a picture here, for at any time, at the right time, in His time, God can raise Himself up in such a way to judge His enemies, your enemies and so in turn, deliver you.

Selah. Think about this tonight. Take an interlude to consider this: No empire, no nation, no government, no gang, business, organization or person can resist the redemptive purposes of God. Look now! All who have stood against Him are gone, long gone. Remember, God comes

> *No empire, no nation, no government, no gang, business, organization or person can resist the redemptive purposes of God*

in a moment and the world is changed! Indeed, if God is leading you out of a situation then the sea shall open to let you out! And if God is leading you into a place, then the rivers shall open to allow you passage! No matter what the noise or crashing tumult, just watch for the openings, the exit and the entrance, and then walk through them, out of your bondage and into His promises. Even if a wilderness lies between the two dear friend, then even there shall you be provided for and even there the enemy shall fall before you.

Remember, that God is a man of war and when He raises Himself out of the sea and bares His bow and fingers round the lid of His quiver, be sure it is for the judgment of His enemies and be sure it is for your deliverance also. Amidst the turmoil, let such a knowledge bring you peace.

Listen: *Then Moses and the children of Israel sang this song to the Lord, and spoke, saying: "I will sing to the Lord, For He has triumphed gloriously! The horse and its rider He has thrown into the sea! The Lord is my strength and song, And He has become my salvation; He is my God, and I will praise Him; My father's God, and I will exalt Him. The Lord is a man of war; The Lord is His name. Exodus 15:1-3 NKJV*

Pray: Make a way O God where yet I see no way. Place me, my Lord, in the chariot of Your salvation and make an exit Lord, yes, break down the walls and make an unprotected breach for me. Yes, make an entrance Lord as well, yes, part the raging and uncrossable river, stand the waters up in heaps that I might safely pass through with You and right on over to cities and the vineyards, to the fields and the corn prepared by Thee for me. Place me, my Lord, in the chariot of Your salvation and then ride on in victory. Amen and let it be so.

Bible Insight 47

Word!

At the beginning of the 21st century, Habakkuk's picture of God as a strong man armed and unsheathing and then unleashing His weapons upon His enemies, is not a picture that sits well with the surrender of affability, and of the current kind of respectable niceness of the church. Even so, the Word of God paints the picture true, and for those of us in the trenches, for those of us pushing hard against the gates of hell, such a picture is a blessing and a comfort. For in this fray, we take great consolation that God can find a way, yes and that God can even make a way where there is no way, to deliver us from all the pressing encirclements of our dirty and dastardly most devilish foe. Christian soldier, remember that God did not deliver you once, twice and three times more, only at last to let you fall into the all-consuming torturous hands of the enemy. Look to Him now! For God is still in the business of the deliverance of His people and especially of His forces all pressing ahead against the falling gates of Hell

Habakkuk 3:9

Thy bow was made quite naked, according to the oaths of the tribes, even thy word. Selah. Thou didst cleave the earth with rivers.KJV.

These covenant promises, these repeated oaths, filter down through Adam, Abraham, Isaac, Jacob, Moses, Joshua, David and a few more folks besides and ultimately find their fruit and flower in Jesus the Son of God, our Lord and Savior, in whom all the promises of God are 'yes' and 'let it be so'. All His promises made to those who belong to Him are ours for the taking, for the utilizing and especially for the making of war. His arrows of judgment and deliverance are put on the wing for our protection today! Remember Christian, that God is the same, yesterday, today and forever.

In the cool current US suburban vernacular, the term 'Word' has come to be an affirmation of spoken truth, or an agreement with truth, and even an underlined fluorescent yellow highlighted affirmation of that which has been told. "Word." In our text for tonight, the KJV rightly leaves us with the same kind of underlined, yellow highlighted, bold embossed italicized and seen from a satellite declaration of God. "WORD!" The Hebrew is 'omer/amer' and John Calvin wonderfully unpacks for us the full intent of its usage here, explaining: "We now then perceive what the Prophet meant by adding 'amer', the word. 'O Lord, thou hast not given mere words to and people; but what has proceeded from thy mouth has been found to be true and valid. Such, therefore, is and faithfulness in thy promises, that we ought not to entertains the least doubt as to the event. As soon as thou givest to us any hope, we ought to feel assured of its accomplishment, as though it were not a word but the exhibition of the thing itself.' In short, by this term the Prophet commends the faithfulness of God, lest we should harbor doubts as to His promises."

People are fickle, and even the best of people will probably fail you.

People are fickle, and even the best of people will probably fail you. Things change for them, circumstances change, time moves on, they have to take care of themselves or their own, or maybe even they have decided to get married, or they have chosen to buy a cow or been led to build some better barns instead. Whatever it is, you get the picture. Hopes, desires, suggestions, intentions and even promises, are often justified by change and moved into un-fulfillment, and you are left hanging. Let us be careful then where we ultimately place our trust. Remember this tonight though Christian, that all that God has said regarding your deliverance and your protection and your provision is unchanging and true. "Word!" "even thy word. Selah!" And that my friends, is the stamp of quality assurance that you can bet your mission and your life on. Now, don't you dare forget it! "Word!"

Listen: *But as God is faithful, our word to you was not Yes and No. For the Son of God, Jesus Christ, who was preached among you by us — by me, Silvanus, and Timothy — was not Yes and No, but in Him was Yes. For all the promises of God in Him are Yes, and in Him Amen, to the glory of God through us. 2 Corinthians 1:18-20 NKJV*

Pray: Lord help me to hear Your word, trust in Your promises and please You with my faith. Amen and let it be so.

Bible Insight 48

Of belly bubbling in the desert

How did the irresistible God manifest Himself among His redeemed wilderness wandering people? Habakkuk, reminds them that God: "divided the earth with rivers."

Habakkuk 3:9-11

......You divided the earth with rivers. The mountains saw You and trembled; The overflowing of the water passed by. The deep uttered its voice, And lifted its hands on high. The sun and moon stood still in their habitation; At the light of Your arrows they went, At the shining of Your glittering spear. NKJV

In Israel's desert wanderings, we have four distinct records of 'miraculous' or 'spiritual' or the immediately 'supernatural' provision of water by God for His people: 1) Exodus 15:24-25; Where a tree was cast into the bitter waters of Marah to make them sweet to drink. 2) Exodus17:6; At the beginning of the dessert wanderings where the rock was struck to make the waters flow. 3) Numbers 20:8; where after the forty of wandering they were ready to enter into the promised land, and where the rock which should have been spoken to was struck twice to Moses's temporal loss, and finally in 4) Numbers 21:16-18 Where water was 'sung up' out of the ground.

Now then, it is that second particular incident which "divided the earth with rivers." In other words, when water was miraculously furnished from the high point of Horeb, that great flow gushed down the mountain and into several tributaries maybe as it flowed out to the red sea. It is my opinion that just as the deliverance from Egypt and the passage of the Exodus was a miracle, yes, just as the presence of the fiery and cloudy pillar was a miracle, and the longevity of their continuing clothing and shoes never wearing out was also a miracle, yes, just as the daily provision of Manna was a miracle, then so was the daily provision of water for maybe just over two million people!

I don't believe the rock literally followed them but the water from the rock did just that. Indeed, as they followed it, it followed them and even if God led them away from this seen running river of life, they could speak to the rock in another place and have the waters flow. Indeed, it was as the leaders, directed by the lawgiver, dug the ground, that Isreal sang up the unseen flow from beneath the earth and pulled out what was needed from the now opened wells to quench their dessert thirst. In this way, in the dessert the rock followed them wherever they went and more importantly, for their wanderings, God cleaved the earth with rivers.

> *,In the dessert the rock followed them wherever they went and more importantly, for their wanderings, God cleaved the earth with rivers.*

If God took care of His people who in their rebellion were waiting to die in the dessert, then how much more would God be able to take care of His people soon to be carted off to Babylon? The remnant of Judah needed to remember that the waters of God's life would reach them even in Babylon. Yes, though there would be rivers in Babylon where they would weep over their remembrance of Jerusalem, where they would be taunted to sing the joyous songs of the Lord by their enemies, yet even there, the hidden rivers of God would also flow below the ground of their captivity and water them with supplies of spiritual life.

Christian in your present distress, in your dessert place, in your barren place, in your place of home sickness and hunger, there is a song of faith for you to sing tonight. Here it is:

Listen: *"Spring up O well," All together now, "Spring up O well." Another time now, "Spring up O well." All together now, until it flows. "Spring up O well" . See, Numbers 21:17*

Pray: Lord you have said: "I will never leave you nor forsake you." So "Spring up O well." Lord you have said: "he who believes in me, out of his belly shall flow rivers of living water. So, "Spring up O well." Lord, they drank of a spiritual drink from a spiritual rock which followed them. So "Spring up O well." Lord, blessed is the man who walks not in the counsel of the ungodly, nor stands in the path of sinners, nor sits in the seat of the scornful; but his delight is in the law of the Lord, and in His law he meditates day and night. So, "Spring up O well." Lord, that man shall be like a tree planted by the rivers of water, that brings forth its fruit in its season, whose leaf also shall not wither; and whatever he does shall prosper. So, "Spring up O well!"

Bible Insight 49

God's majestic ways among the badgers

Habakkuk continues here to remind his soon to be carried away people, of how God had dealt with their enemies in the past. So, again, Habakkuk says that eventually, the sword of God's judgment against them would also be severely judged and destroyed.

Habakkuk 3:10,11

... ...You divided the earth with rivers. The mountains saw You and trembled; The overflowing of the water passed by. The deep uttered its voice, And lifted its hands on high. The sun and moon stood still in their habitation; At the light of Your arrows they went, At the shining of Your glittering spear. NKJV

Nature, like a barking dog at the arrival of its master, like an excited puppy, like a roaring lion, a neighing stallion, a charging rhino, raises itself up at God's presence and runs at His command. Nature is personified when the presence of God appears, even writhing and moving out of the way of His holiness, even the underground rivers raising their hands toward His footsteps on the earth, His riding in the clouds. There is no doubt that wild nature responds to God and is harnessed by Him for His purposes of salvation and judgment. Deborah and Barak give testimony to this when God unleashes His secret weapons of mass destruction: Hailstones!

Nowadays of course, the mere suggestion that the God of all creation utilizes creation in judgment is laughed at and ridiculed. Yet what we have seen in devastation of floods and tornadoes of hurricanes and wild, wild haboobs, are nothing compared to what is to come upon us, the cattle stampede of nature in all its unstoppable force, run on by the heavy horse-backed angels of God all firing their guns in the air. Christians sing to the "Lord of all creation of water earth, and, sky" but effectively in the way they live and talk, deny His immanent presence in it and His absolute and immediate control of it. To the modern Christian, God is 'beyond our galaxy' somewhere, sat in a remote control room, monitoring things. Here a tweak, there a tweak, everywhere a tweak-tweak, but not imminent and in constant control, not near and directing. To the Hebrew, however, God was near, riding on the back of His Cherubim, tumbling through the cumulus clouds; the tops of the mulberry trees shaking when the armies of God passed over them to battle; raining on one city and then allowing drought in another; sending the rains, the former and the latter and withholding them should He so desire. Yes, to the Hebrew, I wonder if God seemed like a muscle bound and shimmering sweaty rider, balancing atop a pair of rampaging stallions, one foot on each back, their reins in His screaming bare teeth, whilst wielding a wild whip in one hand and a sharp spear in the other?

God produces the raindrop and then guides it on its course from heaven to earth, the forces of its surface tension and even the pin prick landing spot in some unknown field, in the middle of an unknown night. Yes, all of this is known and directed by Him

God was so present to the Hebrews in nature, you see, that Joshua of old could call for the sun and the moon to stand still in the skies until he dealt with his enemies, and that greater Joshua in the New Testament could call for the wind and the waves to be still and in an instant, both would lay flat calm alongside His boat, lying like a dog on its back, legs in the air exposing its tummy to be scratched. Listen Christian: God did not spray paint His image on nature and then walk away from it! Creation is His and responds to His imminent presence. God is not nature, but every part of it is known and utilized by Him and is moved by Him to His Sovereign purpose.

Tell me then dear friend, how imminent is Your God? How are His glittering spears striking the earth near you today? Where and to what purpose? How involved in the present storms of your life do you think God is? I tell you, God produces the raindrop and then guides it on its course from heaven to earth, the forces of its surface tension and even the pin prick landing spot in some unknown field, in the middle of an unknown night. Yes, all of this is known and directed by Him.

Bow down and worship Him.

Listen: *Bless the Lord, O my soul! O Lord my God, You are very great: You are clothed with honor and majesty, Who cover Yourself with light as with a garment, Who stretch out the heavens like a curtain. He lays the beams of His upper chambers in the waters, Who makes the clouds His chariot, Who walks on the wings of the wind, Who makes His* *angels spirits, His ministers a flame of fire. You who laid the foundations of the earth, So that it should not be moved forever, You covered it with the deep as with a garment; The waters stood above the mountains. At Your rebuke they fled; At the voice of Your thunder they hastened away. They went up over the mountains; They went down into the valleys, To the place which You founded for them. You have set a boundary that they may not pass over, That they may not return to cover the earth— Psalms 104:1-10 NKJV*

Pray: Lord, send the springs into our valleys; let them flow among the hills. As you satisfy every beast of the field even the wild donkeys with the quenching of their thirst, so satisfy us. As you provide a shelter for the birds of the heavens in the branches and boughs of Your trees, so give us shelter and appointed place where we may dwell. Fill us with a new song, that we would sing among Your branches and satisfy us with the fruits of Your earth and pour in us the wine of Your love that we might be satisfied. Strengthen us with the bread of heaven, anoint our faces with the oil of Your gladness, fill us with Your goodness and set us high in the cleft of Your rocks that we might observe Your majestic ways among the badgers, the noon day sun and the wonders of Your midnight skies. Amen and let it be so.

Bible Insight 50

'Lex Talionis' and the 'long nose' of the Lord

Prophecy regarding the future finds its roots in the practices of the past. So here, whilst these verses apply broadly to the deliverance of Israel from Egypt and their following conquest of the land promised to them, it also seems to reach forth to the fall of Babylon and the fall of every other kingdom set against Christ, before the coming of the one and only, heaven anointed King!

Habakkuk 3:12-13

You marched through the land in indignation; You trampled the nations in anger. You went forth for the salvation of Your people, For salvation with Your Anointed. You struck the head from the house of the wicked, By laying bare from foundation to neck. Selah

NKJV

Certainly Moses was God's 'anointed' to deliver Israel out of Egypt. Certainly Joshua was God's 'anointed' to deliver Israel into Canaan. Certainly David and his house were God's anointed to establish the people of His presence in the land, but more than this, and more than all that, Jesus is God's anointed Son who has conquered Satan, crushing his head at Calvary and who over the last two thousand years has been removing the walls of his fallen kingdom, brick by judgment burned brick, right down through the head removed neck of its remaining walls, to the tops of its very foundations, which shall also soon and very soon, be removed forever! Note this: The salvation of God's people means the crushing of their enemies underneath His bone breaking steps, underneath His angry and crushing, grinded powder making feet. When it comes to judging sin, our God is still an angry God.

The Bible says that the Lord is slow to anger, that is, is 'long nosed' in becoming angry. I like that. It is like saying that from touching the tip of God's long nose, it is a long way before you get to His so very sharp teeth! Ah, but when you do get to the mouth of God's sharp anger, you will find that God's big long nose is now flaring in deep breathed, muscle-primed power. God is slow to anger, yes, however, when He 'kicks off' you had better get out of the way, for He is fierce in His rampaging rage.

What makes God's anger so powerfully and pointedly destructive, and frankly, so very hard for us to sometimes understand, is that it is not driven by frustration nor vindictiveness, neither by tiredness, nor by hatred, nor by wild and selfish incandescent rage either. No, God's anger, the outworking of which is His wrath, is triggered by consistent and arrogant disobedience, and is driven by pure and righteous holiness.

God's anger against sin, sinfulness and sinners, is therefore legitimate, retributive, calculated, specific, pointed, targeted, irresistible, unstoppable and unremitting.

God's anger against sin, sinfulness and sinners, is therefore legitimate, retributive, calculated, specific, pointed, targeted, irresistible, unstoppable and unremitting. It is terrifying! So much so, that even in this age of grace, and especially to the chagrin of the much misguided modern day church, the wrath of God still rests on those who have not believed in Christ as their Savior.

"He who believes in the Son has everlasting life; and he who does not believe the Son shall not see life, but the wrath of God abides on him." John 3:36

God is love. But He is not nice. God is merciful but He is not mental in overlooking sin. God has a 'long nose' but He remains vengeful and is rightly apportioning out His justice, an eye for an eye and a tooth for a tooth. Note as well then, that the New Testament does not lay aside retributive justice, no, for whilst it is now the duty of Christians to personally forgive those who do them injury and harm and to love them, it is still the duty of God and of his agents in government and law to publicly punish those who do such harm and evil. Yes, whilst it is the duty of Christians to personally forgive those who do them injury and harm it is, as much as is in their power, also their responsibility to protect themselves and their families from such harm. So then government and law as agents of God have also the public duty to protect those who 'do good' by punishing those who do evil, and protecting its citizens from such evil, even if it means going to war.

God, in righteous indignation, in much aggravated anger, yes, here in well provoked outrage, is pictured stomping across the earth and crushing His fallen enemies beneath His feet. When we find God striding in such a manner across the scorched hills of our own lands, then all we can cry is "Lord, in Your wrath remember mercy."

Where mercy is 'negative' in that it withholds from us that punishment which we deserve to receive, grace is 'positive', in that it goes on to give us that which we most definitely do not deserve! God's grace is His 'unmerited favor to undeserving sinners' you see, so as Christians, believing that the sinless Son of God died for our sins on Calvary's cross, and took upon Himself the full retributive punishment from God for our sins, we also then freely receive from Him not only forgiveness, but adoption into His family and all that pertains to such a loving and legal transaction. All of this we attained by the grace of God, when we believed that Christ died for our sins and believed appropriately, even appropriatingly, by trusting in Him to save us.

> *God is a God of righteous holiness, of anger, wrath and vengeance. He judges nations, communities and individuals.*

God is a God of righteous holiness, of anger, wrath and vengeance. He judges nations, communities and individuals. Let us cry out for mercy when He unloads His wrath, but more than that, let us be found in Jesus, covered in grace, forgiven and adopted into His family, free to sin no more.

Listen: *For when we were still without strength, in due time Christ died for the ungodly. For scarcely for a righteous man will one die; yet perhaps for a good man someone would even dare to die. But God demonstrates His own love toward us, in that while we were still sinners, Christ died for us. Much more then, having now been justified by His blood, we shall be saved from wrath through Him. For if when we were enemies we were reconciled to God through the death of His Son, much more, having been reconciled, we shall be saved by His life. Romans 5:6-10NKJV*

Pray: Lord, in Your wrath remember mercy and in the grace that is in Your Son, Jesus Christ my Lord, come reconcile Yourself to me. Amen and let it be so.

Bible Insight 51

Reality checks

T he sense of this verse begins with an acknowledgement of the fact that God can, does, and often will cause the enemies of the people of God to turn their weapons upon themselves, (Judges 7:22). The quivering fear of death and the madness of blind desperation which in war can quickly come upon a people, releasing the darkness of the deep sin in humanity which in a short time produces unimaginable horrors. From Russia to Rwanda, the last century alone is testimony to that singular terror which is humanity.

Habakkuk 3:14

You thrust through with his own arrows The head of his villages. They came out like a whirlwind to scatter me; Their rejoicing was like feasting on the poor in secret. NKJV

Note that collective evil has its head and the head has its body of collective evil. Hitler could not exist without the Nazis and the Nazis could not exist without Hitler. The two feed off each other and so much so, that the head and the body become an expression of each other.

Pharaoh was the expression of the vindictive nastiness of his people and his people had become the expression of Pharaoh's own black heart and it is, of course, Pharaoh of old that typifies the anti-God bondage pitted against the people of God. It is he who gathered his army like a whirlwind gathers up the dust and raced across the ground against a seemingly trapped unarmed, untrained and fearful Israel to consume them in joy. "The enemy said, 'I will pursue, I will overtake, I will divide the spoil; My desire shall be satisfied on them. I will draw my sword, My hand shall destroy them.' " Exodus 15:8 NKJV Yet, as Israel escaped from their exultant devouring, it was the sea which ate up savage Egypt and no doubt in the panic of an attempted retreat, their own weapons of war were turned upon one another.

Note as well, that darkness, when it is fully released from within humanity, consumes with a savage and exultant joy about it, even a nasty and mad happiness, even the insane and smiling madness of the joker from the pack. Countless times in the Scriptures, the great fear of a pursued people is to fall into the hateful hands of their enemies. The inquisition, the mad Muslims, the Japanese, the Gestapo, the SS, and ten thousand more gangs of evil thugs all give testimony to that bottomless pit of evil possibility which is humanity.

Habakkuk the seer, within his head had already witnessed this vile madness overflowing the walls of Judah. He had seen the cannibalism, the red stained brickwork of baby brain splattered walls, the gang rapes and ten thousand evils more besides, and no wonder then his simple all-conclusive prayer was that 'God in His wrath would remember mercy.' The remembrance of this particular verse, however, which Habakkuk wanted to leave with the remembering remnant was this: that even this insane and exultant evil, so manifest in the head, so manifest in the mob, so manifest in each and every individual soldier, yes, even this madness could yet be turned in consuming power upon one another.

He had seen the cannibalism, the red stained brickwork of baby brain splattered walls, the gang rapes and ten thousand evils more besides, and no wonder then his simple all-conclusive prayer was that 'God in His wrath would remember mercy.'

Allow me one final comment now on this terrible verse by examining what some may call a milder manifesting of the joy of this darkness released in humanity which is this: 'The rich - feasting on the poor in secret.'

As I write this Bible insight at the beginning of the 21st century, the West has never had it so good. Yet the comparative gap between rich and poor grows wider each and every day, and the mega-rich are running all the global show. It seems to me that the media dumbed down populace, kept in a daze by dope, video games, TV soap operas and short skirted silicon filled reality shows, are being used and utilized like dumb animals. While the mantra of 'we are all in this together' gets mouthed by the rich, it is grossly evident that 'The rich – are feasting on the poor in secret', yes, they are laughing up their sleeve. Remember though and consider, that when the mooing gets too loud in the overcrowded poorer pasture lands, the rich always cull their cattle in the end.

Listen: *Now Harbonah, one of the eunuchs, said to the king, "Look! The gallows, fifty cubits high, which Haman made for Mordecai, who*

spoke good on the king's behalf, is standing at the house of Haman."
Then the king said, "Hang him on it!" So they hanged Haman on the
gallows that he had prepared for Mordecai. Then the king's wrath
subsided. Esther 7:9-10 NKJV

Pray: Lord, deliver us from the hands of evil men. Lord, do not allow us to fall into their hands. Lord, turn insane savages in upon themselves that they might consume one another in their madness. Deliver us from the bondage of drugs and utter nonsense. Give us sanity, give us wisdom, give us hope in You and give us this day our daily bread. Amen and let it be so.

Bible Insight 52

Pharaoh's Ford v God's Ferrari

A gain, Habakkuk continues with His reference to the people of God's deliverance from Egypt and the ever pursuing anti-God Pharaoh.

Numbers 11;29,30

Habakkuk 3:15

You walked through the sea with Your horses, Through the heap of great waters. NKJV

Imagine the fleeing Israelites arriving at the sea. Now then, look at the sea before them. Look at that great water which held them captive in the kill zone. Yet, it was God who would part these same blocking waters and raise them up in heaps to allow the people of God a passage way of safety through to the other side, and then use the same now presently connected and constricting waves of passing impossibility to crush their enemies. Look now! God can take all of our hindrances and blockages, everything that pens us in, and make a way for us through them into safety and at the same time, use those same hindrances to annihilate our enemies!

Look again at the miracle here. The parting of the waters and their standing up and remaining up, was contrary to the natural course and actions of things. God either changed the nature of this water or parted them and held them in their place with some unseen force like the congealed glass sides of some great aquarium? God can make even a great and immovable natural object act contrary to its nature to allow the deliverance of His people from death, yes, and allow them to continue on their journey. God will move the seas to get you where you need to be.

Look again at the imminence of God in this deliverance, yes, observe God's very presence in their deliverance. Habakkuk says that God Himself was with the Israelites, leading them, walking orderly through the dry land passage way of the sea. As Pharaoh raced like a manic madman to pursue and devour his foe, God in His own time, at the right time, without haste, calmly and purposefully, in His mounted chariot moved His prancing horses forward, whose skipping hooves then touched and parted the waters, trampling them down as on He went, moving them to the side as He made His way through. This is no poetic metaphor for the great wind moving upon the water to congeal it in jelly like walls, for just as the fiery and cloudy pillar had 'got their back', God Himself had now got their front, going before them, parting the waves, leading them on.

Dear Christian, that God can move a sea to make a way for thee, and when He does, He does it personally

I wonder if Habakkuk took comfort from looking at the past and that he was from this comfort also reminded that when God's wrath had passed over them, and when their time in Babylonian captivity had been rightly served, that God Himself would ride once more at their head and lead them back the land of His promise?

Remember tonight though dear Christian, that God can move a sea to make a way for thee, and when He does, He does it personally. God is intimately involved both with your protection and with your deliverance.

Look for the sign of the prancing horse!

Listen: *The waters saw You, O God; The waters saw You, they were afraid; The depths also trembled. The clouds poured out water; The skies sent out a sound; Your arrows also flashed about. The voice of Your thunder was in the whirlwind; The lightnings lit up the world; The earth trembled and shook. Your way was in the sea, Your path in the great waters, And Your footsteps were not known. Psalms 77:16-19 NKJV*

Pray: Father, come now and deliver me from every bondage and blocking mountain. Come dance upon my stormy seas and part the waves that I may pass through them to destiny with You. Amen and let it be so.

Bible Insight 53

Doomsday descending

These are the penultimate verses to one of the most majestic hymns of faith ever written.

Habakkuk 3:16

When I heard, my body trembled; My lips quivered at the voice; Rottenness entered my bones; And I trembled in myself, That I might rest in the day of trouble. When he comes up to the people, He will invade them with his troops.
NKJV

I believe Habakkuk knew of Judah's eventual return to the land, but even so, this verse is rooted in a testimony from the rotten 'sick bed' of the seer, and this sickness was his bodily reaction to the visions from God and the soundtrack of His word, and I suppose also, maybe even the presence of the Holy God of judgment in all the utter desolation that was soon to be visited upon His people.

Habakkuk had heard the word of the Lord concerning these judgments and the inner central core of his very being trembled, yes, the heart of him quaked, even the very spirit of Habakkuk shuddered and so much so, that very quickly, this inner trembling grew from direct physiological cause of what was both stark terror and looming fear, outwardly manifesting itself in both Habakkuk's jaw and dry flapping lips, and the dry wood louse crumbling of his once strong skeletal structure. Habakkuk collapsed on the spot and I bet he had to be put to bed. How long he remained there, we do not know, save to say the prophet Daniel would later receive astonishing visions which would make him faint and put him in bed for days. (Daniel 8:27)

Note: It has been my pastoral observation that when the spirit of a man is so opened up, when connection with the inner and outer spiritual realm is so thoroughly established, that there follows extreme physical exhaustion. Preachers must note especially then, that if they are not exhausted on a Monday because of their exertions on a Sunday, then all they have done is talk. They have stayed in the kiddie's pool and waded in the inch high shallows. Mondays are dangerous times for ministers because they are and should be times of utter exhaustion. Listen then flock! Leave your faithful Bible minister alone on Monday. Let him spend the morning in bed and the afternoon at rest. If all he is doing is talking though, then go and bang on his door. He needs praying for.

Habakkuk has seen that 'he' Nebuchadnezzar was invading the land with his troops and what he saw nearly slew him. Like I say however, this verse is nevertheless a preface to the coming great hymn of faith, for something has happened to Habakkuk, yes, in the midst

Habakkuk has seen that 'he' Nebuchadnezzar was invading the land with his troops and what he saw nearly slew him.

of this verse he has found some special rest, for out of the trembling has come a space of peace, even a 'place' within himself where, as Peterson puts it, "Habakkuk now waits in a quiet place for the day of doom to fall upon Judah's attackers". I wonder if that felt rest Habakkuk experienced here was somewhat akin to that strange space of physical resting we also find, when, after a severe drop in our core temperature, our whole body which once caused us to shiver and set our teeth to chattering, has now, by the same shivering raised our internal 'toastiness' to just that right temperature, which then told our brain to 'stop the shivering', and, when that happens, do you recall, when that happens, there are a few moments of heavenly flat calm peace which seems to bring our whole being to rest. Do you know what I mean?

Habakkuk had seen the horrors and heard the word of coming judgment from the Lord, and from his consequent sick bed, had never the less also been reminded of the Lord's past great deliverance of His chosen people and maybe had those same actions of salvation and the destruction of his enemies projected in wide screen high definition onto the white plaster of his own bedroom walls. Now then, with such consolation, Habakkuk's heart had become quite settled on both the great sovereign imminence and the great mercy of God.

Habakkuk had seen the bigger picture, you see. So must we. So must you.

Listen: *What then shall we say to these things? If God is for us, who can be against us? He who did not spare His own Son, but delivered Him up for us all, how shall He not with Him also freely give us all things? Who shall bring a charge against God's elect? It is God who justifies. Who is he who condemns? It is Christ who died, and furthermore is also risen, who is even at the right hand of God, who* *also makes intercession for us. Who shall separate us from the love of Christ? Shall tribulation, or distress, or persecution, or famine, or nakedness, or peril, or sword? As it is written:*

"For Your sake we are killed all day long; We are accounted as sheep for the slaughter." Yet in all these things we are more than conquerors through Him who loved us. For I am persuaded that neither death nor life, nor angels nor principalities nor powers, nor things present nor things to come, nor height nor depth, nor any other created thing, shall be able to separate us from the love of God which is in Christ Jesus our Lord. Romans 8:31-37

Pray: Father, open my eyes that I might see Your greatness and Your purpose, Your chariot and Your horses surrounded me in this great battle. Amen and let it be so.

Bible Insight 54

Six part sanctification

An appreciation of the great testimony of faith and the grand tool of victory found here in 3:18 can only be understood, can only be apprehended, can only be wielded by the bony famine fingers of Habakkuk 3:17! Let's get real here: Habakkuk is speaking of a terrible and most destructive all-consuming war famine, and so this testimony of faith and wielding of the tool of victory is not so much singing often emotionally indulged in church on a Sunday morning, whilst the roast beef and Yorkshire puddings are both bubbling in the hot oven of a centrally heated house, no, this weapon is only really utilized as a tool and declared as a stunning testimony of faith in the face of the very worst of situations. When you can sing and smile and glorify God in the face of disaster, there is a work which will magnify His name and confound the enemy!

Habakkuk 3:17-19

Though the fig tree may not blossom, Nor fruit be on the vines; Though the labor of the olive may fail, And the fields yield no food; Though the flock may be cut off from the fold, And there be no herd in the stalls — Yet I will rejoice in the Lord, I will joy in the God of my salvation. The Lord God is my strength..... NKJV

Habakkuk says here: Though there shall be no blossom, no fruit, no rich red wine; No oil, no bread, no meat, no milk nor clothing neither any seeming temporal provision in the stalls of the future, "YET, I will rejoice in the Lord and joy in the God of my salvation."

Remember now that Chapter 3 of Habakkuk is a six part symphony (Part 1=v2, Part 2=v3-9, Part 3=10-13, Part 4=v14-16, Part 5=v17,18, Part 6=v19) surrounding a great choral dithyrambic, and these closing sections of parts 5 and 6 are probably the most important of the piece because they are God's musical gift of remembrance to the remnant survivors of the wrath to come upon them.

The remnant of faith must remember then, the God of deliverance who will eventually deliver them back to their own land and destroy these terrible invading armies. Such a remembrance will introduce solid steel into their back bone, just as it had this prophet who was able to rejoice and joy in the God of his salvation because the Lord had become His strength, that is, the Lord had become His total source of wealth and supply. Habakkuk knew that when all was gone, God was not gone! God had become to Habakkuk, his all in all.

Such a remembrance will introduce solid steel into their back bone, just as it had this prophet who was able to rejoice and joy in the God of his salvation because the Lord had become His strength, that is, the Lord had become His total source of wealth and supply. Habakkuk knew that when all was gone, God was not gone! God had become to Habakkuk, his all in all

Now then friends, at the time of my writing, this is not my personal story. Even though I have and will be delivered, times of testing just seem to make me stand out like a whining and unthankful former Egyptian slave. I wonder if one aspect of sanctification is that work of the Holy Spirit which strips us of all idolatrous sustenance and provision until we find our wealth that is our strength in the God of our salvation alone. I think it is and accounts for much of our seeming present distresses. Worry not then dear friend, even this is God's work in you to make you rely all the more in Him in the troubled times to come.

Listen: *The Lord is good, a stronghold in the day of trouble; and He knows those who trust in Him. Nahum 1:7 NKJV*

Pray: Father, I kick and I scream. It is no good. Have Your way quickly with me. Spare me no thought, that I soon may stand whole and complete in You. Amen and let it be so.

Bible Insight 55

Of mountain goats and men

Because Habakkuk had found God to become his only source of safety and of sustenance, because the prophet had found God to be his one true source of wealth, and the one true source of his strength and of all supply, his testimony was that God would make his feet like that of a warrior!

Habakkuk 3:19

The Lord God is my strength; He will make my feet like deer's feet, And He will make me walk on my high hills. To the Chief Musician. With my stringed instruments. NKJV

Yes indeed, to be a mighty man of David, a warrior in the army of the Lord, in those days one of the requirements was that you had to be swift and sure of foot upon the mountains, able to speedily pick your way across the rocky terrain and arrive sure footed and ready for the fight as well, even moving from the high hills to the valleys and back again, able to possess the heights of your own homeland against any foe. Habakkuk's testimony was that God had already enabled him to pick his way through the dark terrors of the prophetic word. Yes, God had already brought him through the tremors of seeing terror, to a place of restful triumph. God had given him, not feet to pick about in slough of boggy worry, but 'picking feet' that could at all times find a place to strongly stand whilst traversing all the high hills of battle, and then miracle of miracles, even sing a song of joy whilst doing it!

In the so very troubled times, which shall for the Christian church in the West also become so very full of famine and of invasion, so must we all become men transformed into mountain goats, able to pick our way safely to the front line of the battle, while remaining restful in God, joyful in spirit, settled in His sovereign goodness.

Run by faith then friends, for God is in control. Give silence to your worry and then give great voice to your hope and joy. For your God is the Deliverer, the God of your salvation and the knowledge His glorious person shall indeed cover all the earth, just as the waters cover the sea.

Sing with me now choir:

Listen: *Strike all your stringed instruments you players and sing with me now sweet choir:*

Pray: I shall rejoice in the Lord, for praise from the upright is beautiful. I shall strike up the music of my heart and sing You a new song of joy O Lord; With great skill and glorious well practiced precision I shall play with shouts of joy! For Your word of the Lord is right, and all Your work is done in truth. You loves righteousness and justice and the earth is full of the goodness of You my Lord. By Your word oh Lord the heavens were made, and all the host of them by the breath of Your mouth. You gathers the waters of the sea together as a heap; You lay up the deep in storehouses. Oh, let all the earth fear the Lord; Yes, let all the inhabitants of the world stand in awe of Him. For He spoke, and it was done; He commanded, and it stood fast. The Lord brings the counsel of the nations to nothing; He makes the plans of the peoples of no effect. The counsel of the Lord stands forever, the plans of His heart to all generations. Blessed is the nation whose God is the Lord, the people He has chosen as His own inheritance. The Lord looks from heaven; He sees all the sons of men. From the place of His dwelling He looks on all the inhabitants of the earth; He fashions our hearts individually; He considers all our works. No king is saved by the multitude of an army; A mighty man is not delivered by great strength! A horse is a vain hope for safety! Neither shall it deliver any by its great strength. Behold, the eye of the Lord is on those who fear Him, on those who hope in His mercy, to deliver their soul from death, and to keep them alive in famine. Our soul therefore waits for the Lord; because He is our help and our shield. So shall our heart rejoice in You O God, because we have trusted in Your holy name. Let Your mercy then O Lord, be upon us, just as we hope in You alone. (adapted from Psalm 33)

SO THEN!

This devotional overview of Habakkuk has not been written to simply instruct you or educate you, but rather to jolt you, to move you to get ready for the terrible times shortly to come upon the church. God will not count you as innocent for your lack of preparedness

SO THEN,

GET READY!

THE END

GOOD NEWS FOR ALL SINNERS EVERYWHERE

The Gospel is the good news brought you by the God-man, Yeshua Christ, the Son of God. Your Creator, YHWH, has put His laws for this life and life eternal in His holy Word the Bible, in the heavens, and in your heart. These ten words, these ten commandments are as follows:

1. I am YHWH your God, …You shall have no other gods before me.

2. You shall not make to you any graven image, or any likeness of anything that is in heaven above, or that is in the earth beneath, or that is in the water under the earth, you shall not bow down yourself to them, nor serve them, for I YHWH your God am a jealous God, visiting the iniquity of the fathers upon the children to the third and fourth generation of them that hate Me; And shewing mercy to thousands of them that love Me, and keep My commandments.

3. You shall not take the name of YHWH your God in vain; for YHWH will not hold him guiltless that takes His name in vain.

4. Remember the Sabbath day, to keep it holy. Six days shall you labour, and do all your work, But the seventh day is the Sabbath of YHWH your God, in it you shall not do any work, you, nor your son, nor your daughter, your manservant, nor your maidservant, nor your cattle, nor your stranger that is within your gates, For in six days YHWH made heaven and earth, the sea, and all is in them, and rested the seventh day, wherefore YHWH blessed the Sabbath day, and hallowed it.

5. Honour your father and your mother, that your days may be long upon the land which YHWH your God gives you.

6. You shall not murder.

7. You shall not commit adultery.

8. You shall not steal.

9. You shall not bear false witness against your neighbour.

10. You shall not covet your neighbour's house, you shall not covet your neighbour's wife, nor his manservant, nor his maidservant, nor his ox, nor his donkey, nor anything that is your neighbour's.

OK. First the bad news.

Yeshua, the only begotten Son of YHWH tells us that keeping these ten commands are a matter of the heart, and it is there where they are kept and broken, and so much so, that Yeshua said if a man were even to look with lust in their heart at another man's wife, then that man has committed adultery. All people, have broken these ten words. All people have sinned and come short of the glory of God. God is holy, and there is nothing imperfect in His heaven. Therefore, because of the practical and heart-breaking of any of these ten commands, all people are condemned to hell and lost forever.

Now the very worst of news. This can't be fixed by you.

No amount of good works can make good our sins. No amount of religious rite, can make good our sins, No amount of prayerful intercession or personal sacrifice can make good our sins. We are lost, utterly and totally. The justice and the demand of these broken laws are your eternal death.

NOW THE GOOD NEWS!

Yeshua, the eternal Son of God, clothed Himself in a body and fully became a man, even a perfect human being. Thus, being fully God and fully human, He took the penalty of Your sin, that being death, and paid for it with His own death and now can grant Eternal life to anyone and everyone who comes to Him to ask for forgiveness. This is the Gospel of Yeshua Christ. Only Christianity offer forgiveness of sins through the death of someone else.

This is the word of faith which we preach; That if you shall confess with your mouth the Lord Yeshua, and shall believe in your heart that God has raised Him from the dead, you shall be saved. For with the heart man believes to righteousness; and with the mouth confession is made to salvation. For the Scripture said, 'Whoever believes on Him shall not be ashamed. For there is no difference between the Jew and the Greek, for the same Lord over all is rich to all that call upon Him. For whoever shall call upon the name of the Lord shall be saved. (Romans 10:9-13 NSB)

Rev. Victor Robert Farrell, June 2019 Scotland

A PRAYER TO RECEIVE FORGIVENESS AND LIFE ETERNAL

"Almighty God,

Thank you for sending Your Son to die for sinners just like me.

I believe that He died in my place and took the consequences of my rebellion against You upon Himself.

I am amazed, and so thankful that He suffered the punishment I deserved so that I don't have to.

I am sorry for the wrong I that have done and want to turn from it.

After being crucified for my sin, I believe that Jesus came back to life to prove that He had beaten both sin and death itself, and also to give me new life. This new life I now gratefully receive.

Therefore, please make right my relationship with You O God and send me Your Holy Spirit and let me know that I am forgiven and am Yours forever, and then my Holy Father, transform me from within.

Amen."

Let us know if you have prayed this prayer, and we can rejoice with you and help you achieve the destiny which God has for you!

Email us at vr@66Books.tv

Meet with other believers online at www.66Bible.Church

Bless you!

Have you heard of Night-Whispers?

If you liked the Meta-Physical aspects of Purple Robert then you might just love his 'Everyday Bible Insights' called Night-Whispers. Maybe you need to order a copy?To do this today, simply go to

www.NightWhispers.com

---------------------------0---------------------------

Night-Whispers is written by Victor Robert Farrell, produced by WhisperingWord Ltd. and licenced for the sole use of, The 66 Books Ministry A modern day, Back to the whole Bible, Boots on The Ground, Proclamation Movement. www.66Books.tv

THE MISSION STATEMENT OF THE 66 BOOKS MINISTRY

WWW.66Books.tv | Our Mission is:

1.   "To proclaim Jesus, the Savior of the whole world, from the whole Bible, because He is wonderful!"

2.   Indeed, we are constrained by the love of God, to communicate the rawness of the Bible to real people, in real ways, and our driving and major project of '66Cities' shall take us to the 66 most influential cities of the 250 nations of the world in the next 25 years. That's 16,500 cities!

3.   We are aiming to build relationships with grass roots, real people, that is, ordinary people, who, in their own countries and cities, want to do extraordinary things for Jesus and the Kingdom of God, to bring a Biblical Gospel message that is relevant to now, in a world that has come to believe that Jesus is irrelevant to their lives.

If you would like to partner with us in this great task. Then we want to hear from you! Contact me today on vr@66books.tv

MORE ABOUT 'THE 66 BOOKS MINISTRY'

WWW.66Cities.com | By the year 2047, by the grace of God and according to His will and favor, The 66 Books Ministry shall be preaching consecutively from each of the 66 Books of the Holy Bible, the Gospel of the Lord Jesus Christ in 16,500 of the most influential cities of the world on an annual and ongoing basis!

We do not underestimate the quality teams of trained people that this will take, together with the need for vast amount of materials and finances which will also have to be raised. However, as most futurists indicate that the growing global population will be gathered mostly in major world cities in the coming years, there is a necessity laid upon the church to present and proclaim the God of the whole Bible, through the primacy of preaching in these cities. We are convinced that this is a paramount and pressing concern.

"For since, in the wisdom of God, the world through wisdom did not know God, it pleased God through the foolishness of the message preached to save those who believe" 1 Corinthians 1:21NKJV

"Preach the Word! Be ready in season and out of season. Convince, rebuke, exhort, with all longsuffering and teaching." 2 TimoYou 4:2NKJV

The church is looking for a revival. The 66 Books Ministry, however, is trying to start a revolution of a return to the preached Word, from the whole of the Bible as a precursor to any and all coming revival.

For "whoever calls on the name of the Lord shall be saved." How then shall they call on Him in whom they have not believed? And how shall they believe in Him of whom they have not heard? And how shall they hear without a preacher? And how shall they preach unless they are sent? As it is written: "How beautiful are the feet of those who preach the gospel of peace, Who bring glad tidings of good things!" Romans 10:13-15 NKJV

We are unashamedly looking for and seeking to foster a massive, huge, releasing, transformative, and exceptionally disruptive reversal and revolutionary change, both within the church and then in the world. We are not just another mission trying to do the same as every other mission. We are intent on revolution!

To this revolutionary end, we have no fear of seeming failure and will cultivate that audacious atmosphere within our ministry. We want to attract grass roots people who are people of faith risk takers, for we believe it is people of such life hazarding attitudes that are used by God to make breakthroughs in the world for the Kingdom of God. Hanging back for fear of seeming failure, hanging back and waiting for the trained professionals, both wastes the time of the church time and kills the spirit of victory.

In that spirit then, we therefore are believing that this task can be accomplished by such people within the time frame we have given ourselves.

Fully assured then, that we are in full obedience with the great commission of our great God and Savior Jesus Christ, we do, with great confidence in Him, turn ourselves happily to this so great a task in the hope that, like a happy hound straining at the leash to be let loose, we believe that many other people will smile along with us and be part of this brand new grass roots 21st Century Global City Mission.

If you want to know more and want to be part of what we are doing then go to www.The66BooksMinistry.com or call us in the USA on **855 662 6657**, or email V.R. directly on vr@66Books.TV

AUTHOR BIO | VICTOR ROBERT FARRELL

| Victor Robert Farrell (1960-Now & still alive and kicking) was born in Chesterfield England to Scottish parents with Irish grandparents, which is an obvious recipe for writing and emotional disaster, if ever there was one!

He grew up a culturally excluded Roman Catholic (his parents were divorced,) which is one of the reasons why he hates religion with a passion, and that's an interesting enough fact by itself, because he is also an ordained protestant minister to boot.

V.R. became a Christian whilst serving on board a Polaris Submarine at the end of the cold war. He has gone on to do many things, including being a broadcaster, App developer, performance poet, and the long-time author of 'Night Whispers,' which is read in over 100 counties and is also translated into Spanish (see www.Night Whispers.com)

Currently, V.R. is also President of The 66 Books Ministry: a grass roots global city mission endeavor. I suppose it is this concoction of background and experience which means V.R's communication is always raw and emotive. After all, "If Christianity can be relevant on a Monday morning, several hundred feet underneath an unknown ocean, in a pornographic sewer pipe carrying enough nuclear weapons to destroy a continent, whilst hiding from the Russians, then it can be relevant anywhere and everywhere!"

V.R. sees himself as a servant of the Word of the Lord, and communicating the God of the whole Bible, proclaimed in very real terms, to real people, is both his burden and his passion.

MORNING | **MINOR PROPHETS**

BOOK 38 of 66 | **Zechariah 11**

Signpost Words | **'EGGS OF THE SHEPHERD CLOWNS'**

Highlight Verses | **Zechariah 11:15-17**

And the Lord said to me, "Next, take for yourself the implements of a foolish shepherd. For indeed I will raise up a shepherd in the land who will not care for those who are cut off, nor seek the young, nor heal those that are broken, nor feed those that still stand. But he will eat the flesh of the fat and tear their hooves in pieces. "Woe to the worthless shepherd, Who leaves the flock! A sword shall be against his arm And against his right eye; His arm shall completely wither, And his right eye shall be totally blinded." NKJV

Some Observations |

This chapter speaks of Christ the good shepherd, and finishes with hireling idiots! When Christ was rejected by Israel of old, they got Clown-shepherd hirelings to help them into hell. It is the same today.

Final Reflections |

In this magnificent and prophetic chapter God finishes by asking Zach to dress like a Clown-Shepherd? What does a Clown-Shepherd look like? He has a goatee instead of a full beard. He has his shirt hanging out over his backside. He has a perpetual goofy grin. He is rich, but he has no bread. He cannot heal nor bind up and therefore, he also has no balm from Gilead. He has no rod, and is followed by undisciplined sheep. He has no staff, but in its place a stool. What does a Clown-Shepherd look like? Well, look around Christian, there are many examples to choose from, and each one has an egg with their own garish face painted upon it. Why are we shepherded by Clowns? Because Christ has vomited Laodicea out of His mouth.

THE FELLOWSHIP OF THE BOOK

EVENING | **MINOR PROPHETS**

BOOK 38 of 66 | **Zechariah 12**

Signpost Words | **'THE CRIME SCENE OF THE CROSS'**

Highlight Verses | **Zechariah 12:10-14**

"And I will pour on the house of David and on the inhabitants of Jerusalem the Spirit of grace and supplication; then they will look on Me whom they pierced. Yes, they will mourn for Him as one mourns for his only son, and grieve for Him as one grieves for a firstborn. In that day there shall be a great mourning in Jerusalem, like the mourning at Hadad Rimmon in the plain of Megiddo. And the land shall mourn, every family by itself; the family of the house of David by itself, and their wives by themselves; the family of the house of Nathan by itself, and their wives by themselves; the family of the house of Levi by itself, and their wives by themselves; the family of Shimei by itself, and their wives by themselves; ... NKJV

Some Observations |

So, Jerusalem shall be sieged once more and all nations shall come against the Jews. Then Christ shall come and both strengthen their hands and destroy all their enemies for them. At that point, Israel shall see the nail pierced hands of their Messiah, whom they crucified. Then, they shall repent, and believe, and be saved! Amen!

Final Reflections |

National repentance is made up of broken individuals. Repentance might have a national expression, but in each case, it is of a very singular act. Christian, it is your sin which nailed your Savior to the cross. You have blasphemed Him. You have deserted Him. You have thrust the spear into His side. You denied Him. You despised Him, you used Him & you abused Him. You were at the crime scene of the cross. He remembers seeing you there! Be sure you remember Him dying there for you, so that He might remember you in His Kingdom.

JOIN THE FELLOWSHIP OF THE BOOK

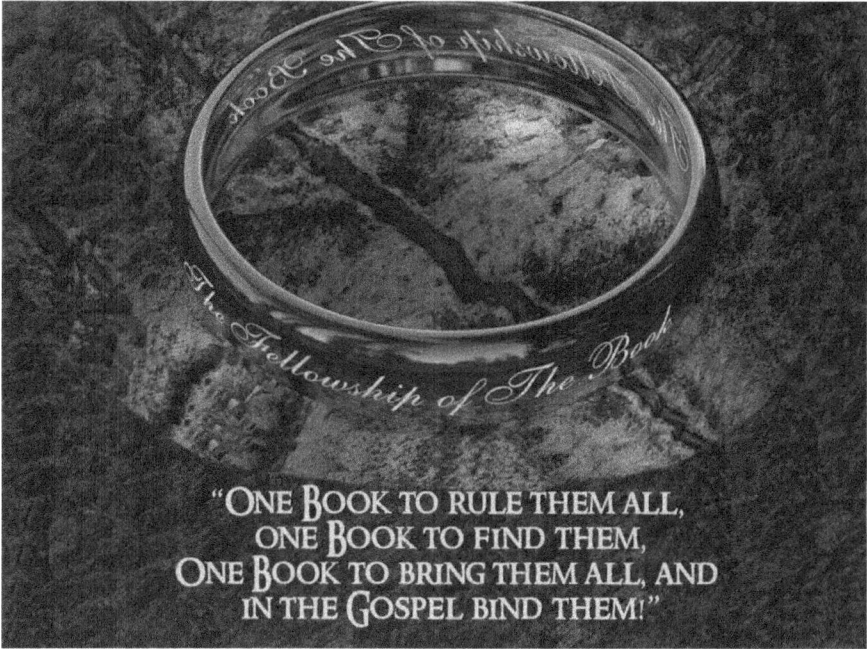

"ONE BOOK TO RULE THEM ALL,
ONE BOOK TO FIND THEM,
ONE BOOK TO BRING THEM ALL, AND
IN THE GOSPEL BIND THEM!"

WWW.TheFellowShipofTheBook.com

The Fellowship of The Book is a Daily Bible Reading Fellowship. You can sign up today and also PRE-ORDER this 738 page Book of 366 Daily Bible Readings with accompanying notes, divided as

Signpost Words
Highlight Verses
Some Observations
Final Reflections

Read The Bible Thru in 1 year, with a Morning and Evening reading to keep your mind focused on the Lord of the Word and the Word of The Lord. Buy this and several other 'Read the Bible Thru in a Year Books' at WWW.TheologyShop.com

ANOTHER BOOK BY THE AUTHOR, VR

Habakkuk A Prophecy For Our Time

As the Church in the West is found to be mostly dead and covered with Laodicean lukewarm vomit, as The Lord, slips the dead things silently over the side of the storm tossed ship into the dark oblivion of the waves of secular humanism and rising Islam, what remains will need to be fortified with steel to live in a quickly changing anti-Christian world of persecution. There is no better prophecy more equipped to speak to such a remnant who shall be so very besieged. Welcome to Habakkuk, 35 of 66, a prophecy for our time.

Buy at WWW.TheologyShop.com

ANOTHER BOOK BY THE COMPILER VICTOR ROBERT FARRELL

The 66-Minute Bible

I am told that there are 788,258 words in the King James Bible and of these 14,565 are unique. That's a lot of words! I have been reading the Bible for nearly forty years on an almost daily basis. It still remains to me the most exciting book on the planet, however, it never gets any easier. Bible reading is a spiritual discipline and for me the emphasis is on discipline. I created this resource to aid you in your Bible reading, it gives your brain a sixty second overview of the Bible, a loose enclosure to herd the narrative of the book into something that can be seen as a whole. It was never created to be a substitute, but an aid. Just saying...... Friends, welcome to the most exciting book on the planet! V.R.

Buy at WWW.TheologyShop.com

THE
NEW SEPARATIST
BIBLE

❦

FOR THE PEOPLE

THE 66 BOOKS MINISTRY & VICTOR ROBERT FARRELL

A BRIEF INTRODUCTION TO THE NEW SEPARATIST BIBLE (NSB)

The New Separatist's Bible (NSB) is a 'Confluence Bible,' and is rooted mainly in the Pure Cambridge Edition of the 1611 King James Authorized Version and shaped by the 1560 AND 1599 Geneva Bibles and 21st century English. It is, therefore, a confluence of these three great rivers, the Authorized Version, the Geneva Bible and modern English. Therefore, the NSB is NOT a translation, it is a confluence. As it brings together these rivers of translation into the 21st century, it is very happily NOT politically correct and NOT gender neutral.

So, just what is the NSB?

The NSB is a Bible is produced with a view to the Non-Christian. It is, therefore, one of a few 'Read & Learn' Bibles rather than a study Bible, and this learning is enabled by the very simple use of copious sub-headings, each rightly dividing the Scripture text into meaningful and instructively headed portions.

In this confluence Bible, I have also decided to use the Hebrew form of Jesus, 'Yeshua' for Son of God, and for the name of God our Father, instead of 'LORD' or 'Jehovah,' I have chosen to use the Holy Name of YHWH.

Lastly, in this confluence NSB, I hope to have retained some of the majesty of language presented in these ancients translations rooted in the received text and with this confluence of compilation I have also tried to fully retain that great 'difference' that is, that great 'otherness' of the received Biblical text, as expressed in the 1560 & 1599 Geneva Bibles and especially the 1611 King James Authorized Version.

And, of course, finally, please note that this confluence called the NSB is in British English.

GET YOURS TODAY AT

WWW.WHISPERINGWORD.COM

& Become a New Separatist at www.TheNewSeparatists.com

AN INTRODUCTION TO 'PURPLE ROBERT'

Some Dangerously Different Devotionals!

Now, before I go any further, this guy comes with warning shots! The opening parts of his currently seven volumes pf poetic works says quite clearly, *"If you are easily offended by low level expletives...**Go no further. Do not read this book!** If you are prudish in any way ...**Go no further. Do not read this book!** If you do not want to be challenged...**Go no further. Do not read this book!** If you want to be stroked into unchanging sleep and into the stupor of remaining as you are...**Go no further. Do not read this book!** If you hide under the respectable covers of a comfortable religion...**Go no further. Do not read this book!** If you are frail in faith and dishonest about life under this sun...**Go no further.** If you have no real integrity regarding the state of your own heart, **then do not read this book!** If however, you are grown up, honest and have a basic human integrity, ENJOY!"*

So, there you go, you have been warned!

Purple Robert is a Performance Poet and a Metaphysical Biblical Realist. If you want to hear some of his work and get hold of the 66 Poems each of the Seven volumes contain, then go to www.PurpleRobert.com and purchase them today.

Also Buy at Buy at www.TheologyShop.com

www.ingramcontent.com/pod-product-compliance
Lightning Source LLC
LaVergne TN
LVHW011225080426
835509LV00005B/320